PRAYERS that BREAK CURSES

JOHN ECKHARDT

Charisma
HOUSE
A STRANG COMPANY

PRAYERS THAT BREAK CURSES by John Eckhardt
Published by Charisma House
A Strang Company
600 Rinehart Road
Lake Mary, Florida 32746
www.strangbookgroup.com

Cover design by Bill Johnson
Design Director: Bill Johnson

Library of Congress Cataloging-in-Publication Data:

Eckhardt, John, 1957-
   Prayers that break curses / by John Eckhardt. -- 1st ed.
      p. cm.
   ISBN 978-1-59979-944-5
   1. Prayers. 2. Blessing and cursing. I. Title.
   BV245.E25 2010
   248.3'2--dc22

                                        2009036111

First Edition

10 11 12 13 14 — 9 8 7 6 5 4 3 2 1
Printed in the United States of America

Contents

Introduction

REDEEMED FROM the CURSE OF BELIAL

D O FAILURE AND frustration seem to be your lot in life? Is your life characterized by continual setbacks and misfortune? Does it appear as though no matter what you do in life, you cannot seem to obtain the blessings of the Lord?

Often the most frustrating thing about this whole scenario is the fact that you are a believer and love the Lord. According to Galatians 3:13, we are redeemed from the curse. In other words, Jesus became a curse in our stead. If this is true, then how can a believer still be under a curse?

Unfortunately, there are still many believers living under curses even though they have been legally redeemed from curses. Just as a believer may have to fight a good fight of faith for healing, he or she may also have to fight a good fight of faith against curses.

Many of the curses that can affect a person's life come as a result of one of the most wicked and vile spirits in the kingdom of darkness—the spirit of *Belial.*

He is a *ruling* spirit of *wickedness.* There is a host of demons that operate under his command, cursing the lives of people, which we will discuss in this book. Belial is mentioned twenty-seven times in the Old Testament and once in the New Testament. It is from the Hebrew word *beliyaal,* which is translated as "Belial" sixteen times in the Old Testament.

This word is also translated in other verses as "wicked," "ungodly," and "naughty." Strong's definition of *beliyaal* is "without profit, worthlessness, destruction, wickedness, evil, naughty." The most common of these definitions is "worthlessness."

Webster's definition of *worthless* is "valueless, useless, contemptible, despicable." *Despicable* is defined as "deserving to be despised: so worthless or obnoxious as to rouse moral indignation."

Therefore, *Belial's work* is to curse men and women, causing them to commit sins that are vile and contemptible. All sin is wrong, and I don't make any excuses or allowances for any sin. However, there are some sins more abominable than others. That is, there are different *degrees* of sin.

Under the Law, there were some sins that were considered "abominations" and punishable by death, while other sins required certain sacrifices. Belial's work is to draw a nation into such abominable sins that it will bring the curse and the judgment of God.

When I observe the practices and sins that are happening in our nation today, I know that the spirit of Belial is behind them. Belial is a strongman in America as well as other nations of the world. Belial is a world ruler of wickedness. Jesus taught us the necessity of binding the strongman in order to spoil his goods (Matt. 12:29). The prayers in this book are meant to do just that—as you pray, Belial, the world ruler of wickedness, will be bound, and his demonic hold on you and on your family and community will be broken.

CHAPTER 1

CURSES CAUSED by the SPIRIT OF IDOLATRY

Certain men, the children of Belial, are gone out from among you, and have withdrawn the inhabitants of their city, saying, Let us go and serve other gods, which ye have not known.
—Deuteronomy 13:13, KJV

THIS VERSE IS the first mention of Belial in the Word of God. The Lord identifies men who attempt to lead His people *away from Him* to serve other gods as "children of Belial" in the King James Version. This passage of Scripture goes on to describe their actions:

> If you hear someone in one of your cities, which the LORD your God gives you to dwell in, saying, "Corrupt men have gone out from among you and enticed the inhabitants of their city, saying, 'Let us go and serve other gods'"—which you have not known—then you shall inquire, search out, and ask

diligently. And if it is indeed true and certain that such an abomination was committed among you, you shall surely strike the inhabitants of that city with the edge of the sword, utterly destroying it, all that is in it and its livestock, with the edge of the sword. And you shall gather all its plunder into the middle of the street, and completely burn with fire the city and all its plunder, for the Lord your God; and it shall be a heap forever. It shall not be built again. So none of the accursed things shall remain in your hand, that the Lord may turn from the fierceness of His anger and show you mercy, have compassion on you and multiply you, just as He swore to your fathers.

—Deuteronomy 13:12–17

"Children of Belial" indicates individuals who were under the control of Belial. They were being used by Belial to draw the people of God away from Him to serve other gods. It is interesting to note that the word *idol* is the Hebrew word *eliyl*, which means "good for nothing, vain or vanity, of no value, thing of nought." This can be summed up in one word—*worthless.*

Belial, which means *worthlessness*, tries to lead men astray to follow something that is worthless. Idols are worthless; they have no value, and they cannot satisfy. There is a principle of Bible study that we call the law of first reference. This law of Bible study says that whenever a subject or a particular word is *first mentioned* in the Bible, there are some important principles that will be found concerning that subject or word.

The *first principle* we see in connection with Belial is that he attempts to draw people away from worshiping the true God. Under Belial are spirits that will *seduce* people and draw them away from the Lord. As a result, the demon spirits operating under the rulership of Belial inflict the people who have been drawn away from the protection of God with bondages and curses that often lead to destruction.

The apostle Paul prophesied, "In the latter times some shall depart from the faith, giving heed to seducing spirits, and doctrines of devils" (1 Tim. 4:1, KJV). To *seduce* means "to lead away, to persuade to disobedience or disloyalty, to lead astray by persuasion or false promises, to attract, to lure." The Living Bible translation of this verse says, "Some in the church will turn away from Christ." This is known as *apostasy.*

Webster defines *apostasy* as "abandonment of a previous loyalty, defection." I believe this is the reason why so many churches and some denominations have abandoned the faith. Some have even ordained homosexuals as ministers. What an abomination! This is no doubt the work of Belial and seducing spirits to cause many to *apostatize.*

CHARACTERISTICS OF THE SPIRIT OF BELIAL

Father, Your Word tells me, "Some worthless people have talked everyone there into worshiping other gods, even though these gods had never done anything for them." You instruct me to "carefully find out if the rumor is true" and call such action "a disgusting thing" (Deut. 13:13–14, CEV). Make me a watchman on the wall to guard against this worthless spirit leading those I know and love astray.

Father, the spirit of Belial causes people "to be so selfish that you refuse to help the poor" (Deut. 15:9, CEV)—even when the poor are their own relatives! You warn me not to be like that and say that if that person I refuse to help tells You of the wrong I do, You "will say that [I am] guilty." Protect me from the spirit of Belial, who makes people so selfish.

God, the spirit of Belial is so perverted that it watches for strangers to visit Your people and then demands that the stranger be given to perverse men and women to satisfy their homosexual lust (Judg. 19:22). Keep me ever watchful, Lord, for those who would be stolen away by the homosexual lusts of

Belial. Make me a strong wall of protection and my home a locked fortress against this spirit.

Your Word tells the horrible story of a traveling Levite who, with his wife, spent a night in the home of a fellow Jew who lived in a city filled with men who were no longer living for God but were filled with the spirit of Belial. These men surrounded the man's home and demanded that the Levite be given to them for homosexual relations. Rather than protecting his wife, this Levite threw his own wife out the door, and she was repeatedly raped by these evil men and died. (See Judges 19.) Lord, teach me to heed the warning of this story and never become so apathetic toward You that I would willingly give up my own family members to evil. Keep me safe in the protection of Your will so that I never stray from You and fall victim or allow my loved ones to fall victim to the spirit of Belial.

Lord, when Hannah was interceding in the temple for a son, she was thought to be a daughter of Belial who was drunk (1 Sam. 1:12–16). Help me to recognize that the spirit of Belial would attempt to bring me under the bondage of some addictive sin that traps me. Help me to recognize these addictive bondages and to avoid anything that could draw me subtly into bondage.

PRAYERS THAT BREAK CURSES

Father, You called the sons of Eli—priests in Your temple—sons of Belial who were living in sin even as they pretended to be men of God (1 Sam. 2:12, kjv). Protect the men and women who have accepted Your calling to ministry, and shield them from the hidden sins that will lead them away from You. Break the power of sin from their lives, and keep them true and honorable shepherds who lead Your people into righteousness.

Father, like Eli's sons, so many church leaders and men of God today have fallen prey to the spirit of Belial and have ended up broken, bound by sin, and unworthy to serve as Your shepherds. Help me to pray and intercede for Your shepherds. Break the power of Belial to lead Your servants astray. Keep them pure and holy and blameless before God and before the people they are leading.

Father, as soon as Samuel had anointed Saul to be king, the spirit of Belial immediately attacked him by casting doubts to the people about his ability to lead them and by their refusing to honor him with their gifts (1 Sam. 10:27). The spirit of Belial was already at work, filling Saul with self-doubt and insecurities about his abilities. Even though he held his peace, this spirit began its insidious attack against him, ultimately leading him to reject You and fail miserably at the job You had called him to. Make me strong against Belial when it tempts me to doubt what You have called me to do or tempts me to feel inadequate or inept. Make me powerful through Your Spirit, and defeat the spirit of Belial from my life.

God, when King David asked the rich man Nabal to share some food with him and his men as they were passing nearby, Nabal was so filled with the spirit of Belial that he refused to give David any food. Even though David and his men had always treated the servants of Nabal kindly and with respect, Nabal sent a rude message back to David, saying, "What makes you think I would take my bread, my water, and the meat that I've had cooked for my own servants and give it to you?" (1 Sam. 25:11, CEV). Lord, may I never become like Nabal! Give me a generous heart and a spirit filled with Your mercy and compassion. Break the power of Belial from turning me into a Nabal.

Father, even Nabal's own wife, Abigail, recognized how sinfully bound he was by the spirit of Belial. She generously fed David and his men and apologized for her evil husband, saying, "Sir, please let me explain! Don't pay any attention to that good-for-nothing Nabal. His name means 'fool,' and it really fits him!" (1 Sam. 25:24–25, CEV). May I never be identified as a fool or a son or daughter of Belial. Protect me from sinful selfishness and stinginess.

Allow me to be an Abigal, not a Nabal, in the way I treat others.

Lord, Your Word teaches that the spirit of Belial can creep in among believers and bind them to sinfulness and evil desires. Even some of David's men were servants of Belial, and David had to rebuke them for being greedy and unwilling to share with those less fortunate than them (1 Sam. 30:22). Reveal any greediness or selfishness in my heart, and break the spirit of Belial from out of my life.

Father, we learn from the example of Shimei that the spirit of Belial will cause us to accuse others of the very sins we have in our own lives. Shimei, one of Saul's relatives, blamed David for the death of Saul and accused him of stealing the kingdom. This man was so possessed by the spirit of Belial that he could not see Your plan and David's commitment to Your plan (2 Sam. 16:7). Father, keep me from being blinded by the spirit of Belial. Reveal my own sinfulness and evil, and keep me from accusing Your children of the ungodly evil tendencies at work in my own life.

Father, Your Word teaches us to deal firmly and permanently with another believer who allows the spirit of Belial to cause him to lead in a rebellion against Your servants. When David recognized that a member of the tribe of Benjamin was inciting a rebellion against him, he took action. He knew that evil spirit could break down the protective spiritual walls around other believers' lives and cause them to fall into evil with Sheba. He pulled his army together and chased after Sheba until he found him and made sure he had been defeated and killed. (See 2 Samuel 20.) Give me the courage to curse the spirit of Belial and destroy it from my life and from the lives of other believers so it cannot tear down the protective spiritual walls around our hearts and lead us into evil.

Father, David recognized that the evil flooding out from the spirit of Belial can cause us to be afraid and swallow us up in the flood of evil (2 Sam. 22:5). When I am afraid and in the midst of "terrible trouble," help me to be like David and to call out to You for help. Protect me from the overwhelming floods of Belial.

Father, help me to recognize the power of Belial and to arm myself with the sword of Your Spirit to fight this evil spirit. It cannot be "pulled up like thornbushes," or "dug up by hand." It requires "a sharp spear" to destroy it and must be "burned on the spot" (2 Sam. 23:6–7, CEV). Keep me from trying to find evil in my own strength. Arm me with Your Spirit and strength, and burn evil from my life.

The spirit of Belial is a lying spirit that accuses Your children and carries out evil plots against them to

PRAYERS THAT BREAK CURSES

destroy them and steal everything that belongs to them. This is revealed in the story of Ahab and Jezebel's plot against Naboth (1 Kings 21). Make me a fearless, courageous servant like Elijah, who was not afraid to confront these evil servants of Belial and to forecast their judgment from God to a horrible death.

Father, when evil Jeroboam and his followers set out to destroy the righteous followers of God, Abijah, king of Judah, confronted him and declared, "God is on our side.... You might as well give up. There's no way you can defeat the LORD" (2 Chron. 13:12, CEV). With God's help, Abijah defeated Jeroboam and the people of Israel who had rebelled against God to become servants of Belial. When Your people today rebel against You and begin to serve Belial, raise up Abijahs who will stand for righteousness and godliness in the midst of apathy and evil. Make me an Abijah, and arm me for the battle for righteousness in America.

Lord, in times of illness and physical distress, keep my eyes focused on You and my heart strong in my faith that You can heal me. The spirit of Belial would try to tell me, "You have some fatal disease! You'll never get well" (Ps. 41:8, CEV). Help me to reject the voice of Belial that would whisper defeat, destruction, and death in my ear. Raise me up to strength and physical wholeness by Your power, and block the tauntings of Belial from my ears.

Lord, "I refuse to be corrupt or to take part in anything crooked." I will not allow the spirit of Belial to take control of my life, and "I won't be dishonest or deceitful" (Ps. 101:3–4, CEV). I will live my life in purity and honor. I will listen only to Your Spirit and will resist the spirit of Belial from entering my life.

Lord, worthless liars who have been bound by Belial go around deceiving others (Prov. 6:12). I will not be one of these worthless liars. I will speak only Your truth, and I will only seek to lead others into the path of righteousness.

Lord, the spirit of Belial destroys the godly value You have given us and causes us to become worthless. Your Word says, "Worthless people plan trouble. Even their words burn like a flaming fire" (Prov. 16:27, CEV). May I never become worthless to You. May I never play with the fire of Belial and become burned by evil. I will not allow the spirit of Belial to destroy my value to You and to others.

Father, Your Word says, "A lying witness makes fun of the court system, and criminals think crime is really delicious" (Prov. 19:28, CEV). Help me to recognize the lying witnesses in America today who mock the godly principles this nation was founded on and attempt to convince others that ungodliness is right. Unmask the spirit of Belial in the voices of those who lobby for ungodly practices and rules, who attempt to water down the righteous principles of this nation and lead us into sinful acts and behaviors. Right the wrongs that have crept into our justice system, into our schools and government, and that are attempting to lead this nation into sinful practices.

Lord, Your Word says that the evil plans a wicked servant of Belial makes against You or Your children are doomed, no matter how strong that evil plan is (Nah. 1:11). I am to keep my eyes on You and not to be fearful of the evil plans of Belial. I will not fear Belial—even when his plans seem too strong to overcome. I will defeat evil through Your power and in the strength of Your Spirit.

God, Your Word says plainly that people who are not Your followers have nothing in common with people who do follow You. You instruct me, "Leave them and stay away! Don't touch anything that isn't clean. Then I will welcome you and be your Father. You will be my sons and my daughters, as surely as I am God, the All-Powerful" (2 Cor. 6:17–18, CEV). I commit myself to You, Lord. I welcome You as my Father. I will not touch the filthy evil of Belial. I will live only for You for all the days of my life.

CHAPTER 2

THE CURSE FROM THE SEDUCTION OF JEZEBEL

Nevertheless I have a few things against you, because you allow that woman Jezebel, who calls herself a prophetess, to teach and seduce My servants to commit sexual immorality and eat things sacrificed to idols.
—Revelation 2:20

BELIAL WORKS WITH *the spirit of Jezebel* to seduce the servants of the Lord into fornication and idolatry. Jezebel can manifest through false teachings and is a seducing spirit.

Again, the intent is to draw people away from the truth and cause them to go into error, causing bondage and curses and bringing upon them the judgment of God.

> Indeed I will cast her into a sickbed, and those who commit adultery with her into great tribulation, unless they repent of their deeds. I will kill her children with death, and all the churches shall know that I am

17

He who searches the minds and hearts. And I will
give to each one of you according to your works.
—Revelation 2:22–23

This was the judgment of the Lord upon those who
allowed themselves to be seduced by the teachings of
Jezebel. Fornication and adultery will always be judged by
the Lord.

Marriage is honorable among all, and the bed unde-
filed; but fornicators and adulterers God will judge.
—Hebrews 13:4

Marriage is under attack in America like never before.
Divorce is no longer considered unacceptable—it is almost
expected. Jezebel is a seducing spirit that draws people
into *whoredom* and *adultery*. This will bring the judgment of God.

Whoredom means prostitution. It also means "faithless, unworthy, or idolatrous practices or pursuits." To
whore means "a faithless, unworthy, or idolatrous desire,
to debauch." Recently, a visiting minister was ministering in our church and began to prophetically identify
spirits operating in our region. As he was prophesying, he
mentioned in the prophecy the spirit of debauchery. I took
note, and the word *debauchery* stayed with me months
after the meeting.

I knew that the Lord, through this prophet, was iden-
tifying a spirit we had to bind in our region. To *debauch*

means "to seduce from chastity, to lead away from virtue or excellence, to corrupt by intemperance or sensuality."

There you have it. Spirits of whoredom, prostitution, and debauchery work under the strongman Belial. *Debauchery* is defined as "extreme indulgence in sensuality." To be sensual means "to be fleshly or carnal, deficient in moral, spiritual, or intellectual interests: irreligious."

It is interesting to note that the only reference to Belial in the New Testament is found in 2 Corinthians 6:15, "What concord hath Christ with Belial? or what part hath he that believeth with an infidel?" (KJV). Paul was dealing with the rampant carnality in the church of Corinth.

Jezebel does not work alone. Belial works with Jezebel to draw people into abominable sins, including sodomy, homosexuality, incest, rape, and perversion of all kinds. Jezebel works through both *manipulation* and *intimidation*. If the spirit of Jezebel cannot manipulate people into sin, then intimation will manifest. Jezebel threatened the prophet Elijah with death. Jezebel hates true apostles and prophets of God.

The greatest threat to Jezebel's influence has always been true servants of God. Those who preach the truth and maintain a standard of holiness are obstacles to the work of Jezebel. This spirit therefore attacks these men and women of God in order to move them out of the way.

PRAYERS

Lord, Your Word teaches that the spirit of Jezebel can masquerade as a person with prophetic giftings and can, therefore, teach and mislead believers to act immorally (Rev. 2:20). Reveal Your true prophets and prophetesses, Lord. Keep Your children from being led into sin by someone who masquerades as a messenger from You.

Father, the spirit of Jezebel is a seducing spirit that is causing rampant destruction in America today. Teach me to "honor marriage, and guard the sacredness of sexual intimacy between wife and husband." May I never forget that "God draws a firm line against casual and illicit sex" (Heb. 13:4, THE MESSAGE).

Father, Your Word teaches the painful lesson of the evil influence of Jezebel. Although King Jehoshaphat loved and served You throughout his life, his son Jehoram, who became king after him, married the daughter of wicked Queen Jezebel. Jehoram was influenced by this evil generational spirit and led his kingdom into worshiping false gods and falling into gross immorality in their lives (2 Chron. 21:11). As a result, You caused him to die of a painful stomach disease. Lord, help us to lead our children into godly marriages and to teach them the consequences of becoming unequally yoked in marriage with the evil spirit of Jezebel at work in a person's life.

Lord, Your children were so influenced by the evil spirit of Jezebel in their king's life that they sinned by committing sexual immorality and engaging in fornication (2 Chron. 21:11). America has fallen prey to this wicked spirit, and our nation is filled with people who no longer live in purity. Cause Your people to make a stand for purity, Lord. Let Your people lead this nation to repentance for its immorality and to turn to You in purity and dedication.

Father, the spirit of Jezebel drives men and women to commit sinful sexual acts because this spirit cannot be satisfied, and it fills men and women with an insatiable appetite for sex. (See Ezekiel 16:23–31.) This sinful spirit has caused brothels to be built where unspeakable evil takes place. It has created the rise of promiscuity in our youth, paid the sinful price of prostitution, and paved the road to homosexuality. In the holy name of God, I bind this spirit and cast it away from this nation. Break the hold of Jezebel from off me, Lord. Loose the captives, and turn me back to purity.

Father, You teach in Your Word, "'Whoever divorces his wife, let him give her a certificate of divorce.'

But I say to you that whoever divorces his wife for any reason except sexual immorality causes her to commit adultery; and whoever marries a woman who is divorced commits adultery" (Matt. 5:31–32). Stop the evil influence of Belial at work in America causing men and women to engage in adulterous relationships and sexual immorality. Belial seeks the destruction of Your divine institution of marriage. Keep me pure in my relationships, and let me join the fight to save marriage in America.

Father, help me to understand that "those things which proceed out of the mouth come from the heart, and they defile a man. For out of the heart proceed evil thoughts, murders, adulteries, fornications, thefts, false witness, blasphemies" (Matt. 15:18–19). Turn my heart toward You, and keep my mouth pure.

Father, teach me the importance of renewing my mind (Rom. 12:2) and of keeping it focused on You. Your Word tells us of those who "did not like to retain God in their knowledge, God gave them over to a debased mind, to do those things which are not fitting; being filled with all unrighteousness, sexual immorality, wickedness, covetousness, maliciousness; full of envy, murder, strife, deceit, evil-mindedness; they are whisperers, backbiters, haters of God, violent, proud, boasters, inventors of evil things, disobedient to parents" (Rom. 1:28–30). I do not want to be like that.

Lord, I know that "the works of the flesh are evident, which are: adultery, fornication, uncleanness, lewdness, idolatry, sorcery, hatred, contentions, jealousies, outbursts of wrath, selfish ambitions, dissensions, heresies" (Gal. 5:19–20). Teach me to live by the power of Your Spirit and to destroy the works of the flesh out of my life.

Lord, You give meaning to my life, and I want to live with You in glory. Help me to follow Your instructions: "Don't be controlled by your body. Kill every desire for the wrong kind of sex. Don't be immoral or indecent or have evil thoughts. Don't be greedy, which is the same as worshiping idols" (Col. 3:5, cev).

Father, "This is the will of God, even your sanctification, that ye should abstain from fornication" (1 Thess. 4:3, kjv). Sanctify me fully, Lord, and let me be totally separated unto You so that evil will not creep into my life.

Father, You wrote to the church at Thyatira, "I know everything about you, including your love, your faith, your service, and how you have endured. I know that you are doing more now than you have ever done before. But I still have something against you because of that woman Jezebel. She calls herself a prophet, and you let her teach and mislead my servants to do immoral things and to eat food offered to idols. I gave her a chance to turn from her sins, but she did not want to stop doing these immoral things. I am going to strike down Jezebel. Everyone who does these immoral things with her will also be punished, if they don't stop" (Rev. 2:19–22, CEV). Examine my heart, Lord, and show me my heart. If the spirit of Jezebel is present in my life, I repent, and I plead for Your forgiveness. And if that evil spirit has somehow crept into my family and influenced my family members with her evil teachings, reveal that to me, and cast it out of my home. I want my love for You and my family's love for You to be pure and holy in Your sight.

CHAPTER 3

THE CURSE OF A SEARED CONSCIENCE

And she wrote in the letters, saying, Proclaim a fast, and set Naboth on high among the people: and set two men, sons of Belial, before him, to bear witness against him, saying, Thou didst blaspheme God and the king. And then carry him out, and stone him, that he may die.... And there came in two men, children of Belial, and sat before him: and the men of Belial witnessed against him, even against Naboth, in the presence of the people, saying, Naboth did blaspheme God and the king. Then they carried him forth out of the city, and stoned him with stones, that he died. Then they sent to Jezebel, saying, Naboth is stoned, and is dead.
—1 Kings 21:9–10, 13–14, KJV

HERE IS AN example of Jezebel and Belial working together. The men of Belial were evidently hired to bear false witness against Naboth. The Living Bible translation says, "Then two men who had no conscience accused him" (v. 13). *Belial causes men to act without conscience.*

Paul further states that there would be those who would be "speaking lies in hypocrisy, having their own conscience seared with a hot iron" (1 Tim. 4:2). The Phillips translation says, "…whose consciences are as dead as seared flesh." The Amplified Bible says, "…whose consciences are seared (cauterized)."

To *cauterize* means "to deaden." One of the ways Belial is able to cause men to commit vile acts is by cauterizing the conscience. Men without a conscience are capable of committing any act without feeling remorse.

Every person is born with a conscience. The enemy must neutralize the conscience before seducing men to commit certain sins. According to Titus 1:15, the mind and conscience can be defiled. To *defile* means "to contaminate or make unclean." This is obviously a reference to evil spirits operating in the conscience.

When the conscience is seared, men and women are opened to all kinds of unclean spirits and their curses and are capable of all kinds of unclean acts. For example, there are many today who no longer feel that homosexuality, lesbianism, and incest are wrong.

Belial has cauterized the conscience to accept these things as acceptable lifestyles. When the conscience has been seared, men are capable of the vilest and most sickening acts. There is almost no limit to the depravity that men can exhibit when they are bound by the curse of a seared conscience.

PRAYERS

Father, like the men who stood ready to stone the woman caught in the act of adultery but who were "convicted by their conscience" and, therefore, "went out one by one, beginning with the oldest even to the last," leaving "Jesus…alone, and the woman standing in the midst," (John 8:9–10), convict me of the sins I try to hide and fail to admit, and bring me to repentance.

Father, let me become like Paul, who "earnestly beholding the council, said, Men and brethren, I have lived in all good conscience before God until this day" (Acts 23:1–3, KJV).

Lord, "I am just as sure as these people are that God will raise from death everyone who is good or evil. And because I am sure, I try my best to have a clear conscience in whatever I do for God or for people" (Acts 24:15–16, CEV).

Father, as a believer, I know, "We have only one God, and he is the Father. He created everything, and we live for him. Jesus Christ is our only Lord. Everything was made by him, and by him life was given to us." But like the apostle Paul, who wrote, "Not everyone knows these things. In fact, many people have grown up with the belief that idols have life in them. So when they eat meat offered to idols, they are bothered by a weak conscience" (1 Cor. 8:6–7, CEV), make me sensitive to others whose consciences are weak and who may still be bound by ritualistic traditions.

Father, Your Word advises me to "be careful, however, that the exercise of your freedom does not become a stumbling block to the weak" (1 Cor. 8:9, NIV). Keep me sensitive to others so that someone else does not get wounded by my actions, for "when you sin against your brothers in this way and wound their weak conscience, you sin against Christ" (v. 12).

Lord, make me worthy of saying, as Paul did, "Our conscience testifies that we have conducted ourselves in the world, and especially in our relations with you, in the holiness and sincerity that are from God. We have done so not according to worldly wisdom but according to God's grace" (2 Cor. 1:12, NIV).

Father, I renounce "secret and shameful ways" (2 Cor. 4:2, NIV). With Paul, I say, "We use no hocus-pocus, no clever tricks, no dishonest manipulation of the Word of God. We speak the plain truth and so commend ourselves to every man's conscience in the sight of God. If our Gospel is 'veiled,' the veil must be in the minds of those who are spiritually dying" (2 Cor. 4:2–3, Phillips).

Lord, keep me from a seared conscience. Let me serve You in honesty and integrity. Like Paul, "since, then, we know what it is to fear the Lord, we try to persuade men. What we are is plain to God, and I hope it is also plain to your conscience" (2 Cor. 5:11, niv).

Father, make me the kind of teacher of Your Word that Paul instructed Timothy to be: "Command certain men not to teach false doctrines any longer nor to devote themselves to myths and endless genealogies. These promote controversies rather than God's work—which is by faith. The goal of this command is love, which comes from a pure heart and a good conscience and a sincere faith. Some have wandered away from these and turned to meaningless talk. They want to be teachers of the law, but they do not know what they are talking about or what they so confidently affirm" (1 Tim. 1:3–7, niv). May everything I do come from "love…a pure heart and a good conscience and a sincere faith" (v. 5).

Lord, let me "fight the good fight, holding on to faith and a good conscience" (1 Tim. 1:18–19, niv).

Father, only if I keep my life pure and protect my conscience from being seared by sin will I be worthy of serving You as a deacon in Your church. If I am given the sacred trust of a deacon, may I follow Paul's instruction: "Deacons, likewise, are to be men worthy of respect, sincere, not indulging in much wine, and not pursuing dishonest gain. They must keep hold of the deep truths of the faith with a clear conscience. They must first be tested; and then if there is nothing against them, let them serve as deacons" (1 Tim. 3:8–10, NIV).

Father, let me say with Paul, "I thank God, whom I serve, as my forefathers did, with a clear conscience" (2 Tim. 1:3, NIV).

Lord, when we come before You, "let us draw near to God with a sincere heart in full assurance of faith, having our hearts sprinkled to cleanse us from a guilty conscience and having our bodies washed with pure water" (Heb. 10:22, NIV).

Lord, help me to call upon the power of intercessors by asking Your prayer warriors to "keep praying for us, for we are convinced that we have a good (clear) conscience, that we want to walk uprightly and live a noble life, acting honorably and in complete honesty in all things" (Heb. 13:18, AMP).

Lord, give me a conscience that is always following in Your footsteps and remembering how You suffered for me. Your Word reminds me, "For it is commendable if a man bears up under the pain of unjust suffering because he is conscious of God. But how is it to your credit if you receive a beating for doing wrong and endure it? But if you suffer for doing good and you endure it, this is commendable before God" (1 Pet. 2:19–20, NIV).

Father, I want to be the kind of Christian who can follow the advice of Paul: "Honor Christ and let him be the Lord of your life. Always be ready to give an answer when someone asks you about your hope. Give a kind and respectful answer and keep your conscience clear. This way you will make people ashamed for saying bad things about your good conduct as a follower of Christ. You are better off to obey God and suffer for doing right than to suffer for doing wrong" (1 Pet. 3:15–17, CEV).

CHAPTER 4

CURSED BY SPIRITS OF INFIRMITY

"An evil disease," they say, "clings to him. And now that he lies down, he will rise up no more."
—Psalm 41:8

IN BIBLE TIMES, fatal diseases were considered a thing of Belial. The Revised Standard version says, "A deadly thing has fastened upon him; he will not rise again from where he lies."

Belial also has a host of spirits of infirmity and sickness that operate under him. Wherever there is immorality, there will be sickness and death. These are curses that come upon those who are perverse and crooked. Remember, Belial desires to draw men into sin, immorality, and perversion in order to bring the curse of the Lord upon a nation.

"Whoremongers and adulterers God will judge" (Heb. 13:4, KJV). It is possible that AIDS is a thing of Belial that cleaves to a person. AIDS is undoubtedly the result of sin, homosexuality, fornication, perversion, and drug abuse. AIDS is fatal, and in the natural, there is no cure. The New Living Translation of Psalm 41:8 says, "'He has some fatal disease,' they say. 'He will never get out of that bed!'"

The context of Psalm 41 is again the attacks of Belial against David, the Lord's anointed. David states, "All who hate me whisper together against me; against me they devise my hurt" (Ps. 41:7). Again, Belial is mentioned in this context. I believe that as an End Time spirit, Belial has been released by the enemy to attack ministry gifts.

These can also include curses of *witchcraft* against true servants of the Lord, which often manifest through sickness. Leaders need strong prayer support against these spirits that are released under the strongman Belial, who hates and seeks to destroy ministry gifts.

PRAYERS

Lord, Your Word promises, "And ye shall serve the LORD your God, and he shall bless thy bread, and thy water; and I will take sickness away from the midst of thee" (Exod. 23:25, KJV).

Father, I want to serve You in honesty and obedience, for Your Word promises, "Because you listen to these judgments, and keep and do them…you shall be blessed above all peoples; there shall not be a male or female barren among you or among your livestock. And the Lᴏʀᴅ will take away from you all sickness, and will afflict you with none of the terrible diseases of Egypt which you have known" (Deut. 7:12, 14–15).

Lord, when You walked on Earth, You "went about all Galilee, teaching in their synagogues, preaching the gospel of the kingdom, and healing all kinds of sickness and all kinds of disease among the people" (Matt. 4:23). Walk today among my family and loved ones, Lord. Heal "all kinds of sickness and all kinds of disease" that try to afflict my loved ones, through Your holy power.

Father, give me faith as strong as the leper who "came and worshiped" You, saying, "Lord, if You are willing, You can make me clean." Your Word says that immediately You "put out [Your] hand and touched him, saying, 'I am willing; be cleansed'" (Matt. 8:2–3). Immediately that leper's disease was cleansed because of his faith.

Jesus, You are the Great Physician. Your life on Earth was filled with miracles of healing. When a centurion asked You to heal his sick servant at home, You said, "I will go and heal him." But that man had enough faith in Your power to heal that he said, "But just say the word, and my servant will be healed." You honored his faith and told him, "Go! It will be done just as you believed it would" (Matt. 8:7–8, 13, NIV). And his servant was healed at that very hour.

Jesus, when You visited Peter's home, You discovered that his mother-in-law was "lying in bed with a fever." You "touched her hand and the fever left her, and she got up and began to wait on [You]" (Matt. 8:14–15). What an awesome healer You are!

Lord, help me to be like those who believed so much in Your healing power that "they brought to Him many who were demon-possessed. And He cast out the spirits with a word, and healed all who were sick" (Matt. 8:16). Truly You are the Great Physician who "took up our infirmities and carried our diseases" (v. 17, NIV).

Lord, in Your infinite wisdom You know that not only our bodies need Your healing touch, but our souls need Your healing too. When a paralyzed man was brought to You for physical healing, You first healed him spiritually by forgiving his sins. Then You told him, "'Get up, take your mat and go home.' And the man got up and went home" (Matt. 9:6–7, NIV).

Lord, when the Pharisees asked Your disciples why You would sit down and eat with tax collectors and sinners, You told them, "It is not the healthy who need a doctor, but the sick. But go and learn what this means: 'I desire mercy, not sacrifice.' For I have not come to call the righteous, but sinners" (Matt. 9:12–13, NIV). Help me to understand that in mercy, You have called me and healed me—physically and spiritually.

Lord, Your healing power is so powerful that it can raise the dead. When You went to a ruler's home and saw that his daughter had died and the crowd was already following their tradition of mourning the dead, You told them, "Go away. The girl is not dead but asleep." You ignored their laughing disbelief, made them go outside, and "went in and took the girl by the hand, and she got up" (Matt. 9:24–25, NIV). I will believe in Your power to heal and raise the dead, Lord, and will not doubt Your Word.

Jesus, when a woman who had suffered with a blood disease for twelve years reached out in faith to touch the edge of Your garment, You saw her and told her, "Take heart, daughter...your faith has healed you." And she was "healed from that moment" (Matt. 9: 22, NIV). Give me faith like her, Lord.

Lord, when two blind men followed You and asked You to heal them, You asked them, "Do you believe that I am able to do this?" They quickly responded, "Yes, Lord," and You touched their eyes and healed them. May I never forget the words You spoke to them: "According to your faith will it be done to you" (Matt. 9:27–30, NIV). Enlarge my faith, Lord, to believe in the impossible!

Lord, You "went through all the towns and villages, teaching in their synagogues, preaching the good news of the kingdom and healing every disease and sickness" (Matt. 9:35, NIV). You had compassion on people and described them as "harassed and help-less, like sheep without a shepherd" (v. 36). Just as then, Lord, "the harvest is plentiful but the workers are few" (v. 37). Send me out as a worker in Your harvest field. Help me to spread the news of Your power to heal and to save.

When You called Your twelve disciples, Lord, You "gave them power over unclean spirits, to cast them out, and to heal all kinds of sickness and all kinds of disease" (Matt. 10:1). Help me to understand that You have called me to be Your disciple and that You have given me the same power to cast out demons—even the wicked spirit of Belial—and to heal sickness and disease.

Lord, You told Your disciples, "Go, preach, saying, 'The kingdom of heaven is at hand.' Heal the sick, cleanse the lepers, raise the dead, cast out demons. Freely you have received, freely give" (Matt. 10:7–8).

I am Your disciple, and I will follow Your command to GO.

Father, help me to understand that I am ministering to You when I serve others. When the disciples asked You, "Lord, when did we see You hungry and feed You, or thirsty and give You drink? When did we see You a stranger and take You in, or naked and clothe You? Or when did we see You sick, or in prison, and come to You?" Your response to them is the same response You give to me: "Assuredly, I say to you, inasmuch as you did it to one of the least of these My brethren, you did it to Me" (Matt. 25:37–40).

Father, You gave a wonderful promise in Your Word for those who believe in You. You demonstrated that Your power was greater than the evil powers of Belial, for You promised to those who are saved, "Everyone who believes me will be able to do wonderful things. By using my name they will force out demons, and they will speak new languages. They will handle snakes and will drink poison and not be hurt. They will also heal sick people by placing their hands on them" (Mark 16:17–18, cev).

Father, give me a spirit like Peter, who, after he was filled with Your Holy Spirit, was so full of Your power that "they brought the sick out into the streets and laid them on beds and couches, that at least the shadow of Peter passing by might fall on some of them" (Acts 5:14–16).

Lord, give me the confidence that Peter had to know that he had been filled with Your power to heal. When he saw a man who had been bedridden for eight years with palsy, he told the man, "Jesus Christ has healed you! Get up and make up your bed." Right away he stood up (Acts 9:34, CEV).

Father, when a wonderful Greek Christian woman in Joppa who "was always doing good things for people and had given much to the poor...got sick and died," the followers sent for Peter to come to heal her. After he sent the mourners out of the room, he said to her, "Tabitha, get up!" When she opened her eyes and saw Peter, she sat up, and he took her by the hand and helped her to her feet (Acts 9:36–41, CEV). This story teaches me to be busy doing good things for others, because You will always take care of me.

Lord, You gave great healing power to Paul, as you did Peter. Your Word tells us, "God gave Paul the power to work great miracles. People even took handkerchiefs and aprons that had touched Paul's body, and they carried them to everyone who was sick. All of the sick people were healed, and the evil spirits went out" (Acts 19:11–12, CEV). Give me Your supernatural healing power too, and let me heal the sick and cast out the spirit of Belial at work in our world today.

Father, Your glorious healing power even protected Paul from the bite of a dangerous snake. He shook that snake off just as we have the power to shake off the spirit of Belial. That was a mighty witness to everyone around, and it gave Paul the opportunity to heal anyone who was sick on the island (Acts 28:3–9). Let Your healing power at work in me be a mighty witness of Your power and glory.

Father, we are commanded in Your Word, "If you are sick, ask the church leaders to come and pray for you. Ask them to put olive oil on you in the name of the Lord. If you have faith when you pray for sick people, they will get well. The Lord will heal them, and if they have sinned, he will forgive them. If you have sinned, you should tell each other what you have done. Then you can pray for one another and be healed. The prayer of an innocent person is powerful, and it can help a lot" (James 5:14–16, CEV).

What a wonderful promise You have given to us, Lord. "Believing-prayer will heal you, and Jesus will put you on your feet. And if you've sinned, you'll be forgiven—healed inside and out" (James 5:15, THE MESSAGE).

CHAPTER 5

THE SPIRITS OF ALCOHOL AND DRUNKENNESS

Now Hannah spoke in her heart; only her lips moved, but her voice was not heard. Therefore Eli thought she was drunk. So Eli said to her, "How long will you be drunk? Put your wine away from you!" And Hannah answered and said, "No, my lord, I am a woman of sorrowful spirit. I have drunk neither wine nor intoxicating drink, but have poured out my soul before the LORD. Do not consider your maidservant a wicked woman, for out of the abundance of my complaint and grief I have spoken until now."
—1 Samuel 1:13–16

IN THE KING James Version, verse 16 says, "Count not thine handmaid for a daughter of Belial." Eli had thought that Hannah was drunk. The spirit of Belial operates through *alcohol* and *drunkenness*. Drunkenness is a way to break down the morals and open people up to *lust*

and *perversion*. I believe that spirits of alcohol and drunkenness operate under the strongman of Belial.

It is a known fact that many children of alcoholic
parents are often the victims of sexual abuse, including
incest. Alcohol can also open the door for *spirits of rape*,
including "date rape" (which is so prevalent on many
college campuses).

Proverbs warns us of the dangers of alcohol:

> Do not look on the wine when it is red,
> When it sparkles in the cup,
> When it swirls around smoothly;
> At the last it bites like a serpent,
> And stings like a viper.
> Your eyes will see strange things,
> And your heart will utter perverse things.
>
> —Proverbs 23:31–33

These verses show the connection of the spirit of perversion to drunkenness. To *pervert* means "to cause to turn
aside or away from what is good or true or morally right,
to corrupt, to cause to turn aside from what is generally
done or accepted."

Sexual perversion has become rampant in our nation
with the promotion of homosexuality and lesbianism as
acceptable and alternate lifestyles. These are *perversions*
according to the Word of God. Spirits of perversion,
including homosexuality and lesbianism, operate under

the strongman of Belial. This is also referred to in the Word of God as *sodomy*.

Sodomy is defined as "copulation with a member of the same sex or with an animal (bestiality)." It is also noncoital, especially anal or oral copulation, with a member of the opposite sex. The term "sodomite" is mentioned five times in the Old Testament.

Sodomites were temple prostitutes who were a part of the worship of the idol gods of fertility in Canaan. These vile acts were a part of the idol worship of the Canaanites.

THE SONS OF ELI

> Now the sons of Eli were corrupt; they did not know the LORD....Now Eli was very old; and he heard everything his sons did to all Israel, and how they lay with the women who assembled at the door of the tabernacle of meeting.
>
> —1 Samuel 2:12, 22

The sons of Eli represent *ministry*. They, along with Eli, were in charge of the priesthood, regulating the temple, and the sacrifices of Israel. Their abuses brought the judgment of the Lord upon them and the establishment of a new order under Samuel. These sons are called "sons of Belial." They were being motivated and controlled by the spirit of Belial.

One of the works of Belial is to bring uncleanness into the temple of God. The ministry is a target of this spirit. He

PRAYERS THAT BREAK CURSES

desires to draw the servant of the Lord, His anointed, into sin (especially sexual sin) to bring reproach to the church.

These priests were also guilty of greed in making themselves "fat with the best of all the offerings of Israel" (1 Sam. 2:29). Their sin was so great that "men abhorred the offering of the LORD" (v. 17).

> If one man sins against another, God will judge him. But if a man sins against the LORD, who will intercede for him?" Nevertheless they did not heed the voice of their father, because the LORD desired to kill them.
>
> —1 Samuel 2:25

The Rotherham translation says, "for Yahweh was pleased to put them to death." The Lord judged their sin with death. There is no reason for this kind of activity, especially from those who are in the ministry. God forbids men of God to lie with the women of their congregations.

The spirit of Belial desires to draw the servants of God into this kind of hideous activity in order to bring curses and judgment upon the servants of the Lord. The sons of Eli "knew not the LORD" (1 Sam. 2:12, KJV). True apostles, prophets, evangelists, pastors, and teachers know the Lord. They also know that there are moral standards by which God's servants are expected to live.

Remember, "whoremongers and adulterers God will judge" (Heb. 13:4, KJV). God told Eli:

44

> For I have told him that I will judge his house forever
> for the iniquity which he knows, because his sons
> made themselves vile, and he did not restrain them.
>
> —1 Samuel 3:13

This verse tells us the Lord considered their acts *vile*. The Berkeley translation says, "His sons were bringing a curse upon themselves." The Revised Standard Version says, "…because his sons were blaspheming God."

Again, the work of Belial is to cause men to get involved in sins that are abominable and bring the curse of God.

> …who, knowing the righteous judgment of God,
> that those who practice such things are worthy of
> death, not only do the same but also approve of
> those who practice them.
>
> —Romans 1:32

What sins does Paul mention that are worthy of death? The answer is *idolatry*, *homosexuality*, and *lesbianism*. Now, I am not stating that every person involved in these sins should be put to death. Thank God for His mercy. There is salvation offered to all. Jesus died and shed His blood for sin. Those who repent and accept His sacrifice will receive deliverance and forgiveness of sin.

However, the judgment of God does come to those who, through a hard and impenitent heart, will not repent (Rom. 2:5). Regardless of what the secular media try to tell us concerning homosexuality and lesbianism, these are perversions and are under the judgment of God.

> For this reason God gave them up to vile passions. For even their women exchanged the natural use for what is against nature. Likewise also the men, leaving the natural use of the woman, burned in their lust for one another, men with men committing what is shameful, and receiving in themselves the penalty of their error which was due.
>
> —Romans 1:26–27

The Phillips translation calls them "disgraceful passions." The Knox version says "disgraceful acts." The Conybeare translation says, "…men with men working abomination."

Webster's definition of *abomination* is "extreme disgust and hatred, loathing." *Loathe* means "to dislike greatly and often with disgust or intolerance, to detest."

> And even as they did not like to retain God in their knowledge, God gave them over to a debased mind, to do those things which are not fitting.
>
> —Romans 1:28

Reprobate spirits also operate with homosexuality and perversion. The dictionary definition of *reprobate* is "rejected as worthless, morally abandoned, depraved." You will recall that the definition of *Belial* is "worthlessness."

When something is reprobate, it has been judged by God as worthless and, therefore, rejected. The Revised Standard

Version says, "God gave them up to a base mind." The word *base* means "to be of little value." Synonyms include *low* and *vile*, meaning, "deserving contempt because of the absence of higher values, disgusting depravity or filth."

Belial is a wicked ruler that leads men into sins that are base and vile. Reprobate spirits and spirits of homosexuality and lesbianism operate under Belial cursing men to commit vile acts, thus bringing the judgment of God.

The apostle Paul goes on to mention a host of evil spirits that come in once the mind becomes reprobate:

> Being filled with all unrighteousness, sexual immorality, wickedness, covetousness, maliciousness; full of envy, murder, strife, deceit, evil-mindedness; they are whisperers, backbiters, haters of God, violent, proud, boasters, inventors of evil things, disobedient to parents, undiscerning, untrustworthy, unloving, unforgiving, unmerciful.
>
> —Romans 1:29–31

These verses say that they are *filled* with these things. This is obviously a list of demons that enter and dwell in those who are guilty of *base sins*. In other words, those guilty of these sins had become demonized.

Unclean sexual acts attract curses from unclean spirits. The only solution is repentance and deliverance.

PRAYERS

DRUNKENNESS

Father, help me to listen to the warning in Your Word to "take heed to yourselves, lest your hearts be weighed down with carousing, drunkenness, and cares of this life." Keep me focused on living for You, so that I am not caught in the devil's snare to cause me to be unprepared when "that Day come on you unexpectedly" (Luke 21:34).

Father, help me to "live and conduct [myself] honorably and becomingly as in the [open light of] day, not in reveling (carousing) and drunkenness, not in immorality and debauchery (sensuality and licentiousness), not in quarreling and jealousy" (Rom. 13:13, AMP).

Lord, I want to do only what You want me to do, for following my own desires will lead me astray. "People's desires make them give in to immoral ways, filthy thoughts, and shameful deeds. They worship idols, practice witchcraft, hate others, and are hard to get along with. People become jealous, angry, and selfish. They not only argue and cause trouble, but they are envious. They get drunk, carry on at wild parties, and do other evil things as well" (Gal. 5:19–21, CEV). I don't want to live like that,

Lord. I want to honor and serve You in everything I do.

Father, You give good advice in Your Word—advice I want to follow: "Oh listen, dear child—become wise; point your life in the right direction. Don't drink too much wine and get drunk; don't eat too much food and get fat. Drunks and gluttons will end up on skid row, in a stupor and dressed in rags" (Prov. 23:21, THE MESSAGE).

Father, Your Word warns me to be careful about the kind of people I hang around with. Help me to heed Your advice to "not associate with anyone who calls himself a brother but is sexually immoral or greedy, an idolater or a slanderer, a drunkard or a swindler" (1 Cor. 5:11, NIV). Help me to choose my friends wisely.

Lord, I do not want to "be drunk with wine, in which is dissipation." I want to be "filled with the Spirit" (Eph. 5:18). Fill me with Your Spirit, Lord.

God, from the time of Aaron, You have instructed Your Christian leaders and ministers: "When you enter the Tent of Meeting, don't drink wine or strong drink, neither you nor your sons, lest you die. This is a fixed rule down through the generations. Distinguish between the holy and the common" (Lev. 10:8–10, THE MESSAGE). May I never fail You by making what is holy, common, by my sinfulness and drunkenness.

Father, You taught that anyone who is "consecrating yourself totally to God" should not "drink any wine or beer, no intoxicating drink of any kind" (Num. 6:2, The Message). Help me to understand that drunkenness destroys my ability to stay consecrated to You, and help me to turn away from that which has the power to turn me away from You.

Lord, help me to follow the simple advice of Your Word, which says, "It isn't smart to get drunk! Drinking makes a fool of you and leads to fights" (Prov. 20:1, cev).

Father, You have strong advice about the dangers of drunkenness for those who are called to be leaders, for in Your Word, You say, "Kings and leaders should not get drunk or even want to drink" (Prov. 31:4, cev). Help me to honor Your Word in this matter.

Lord, help me to understand how easily Satan can trap us in the bondage of alcoholism. It becomes so powerful that it takes over a person's life. Your Word reminds us of this by saying, "You are in for trouble! You get up early to start drinking, and you keep it up late into the night. At your drinking parties you have the music of stringed instruments, tambourines, and flutes. But you never even think about all the LORD has done, and so his people know nothing about him" (Isa. 5:11–13, CEV).

Father, the enemy blinds us to the dangers of drunkenness and alcoholism, and Your Word describes how it affects our actions: "You think you are clever and smart. And you are great at drinking and mixing drinks. But you are in for trouble. You accept bribes to let the guilty go free, and you cheat the innocent out of a fair trial. You will go up in flames like straw and hay! You have rejected the teaching of the holy LORD God All-Powerful of Israel. Now your roots will rot, and your blossoms will turn to dust" (Isa. 5:21–24, CEV).

Father, wake up the spiritual leaders of the world today to understand Your disgust at their drunkenness. Your Word says, "Priests and prophets stumble because they are drunk. Their minds are too confused to receive God's messages or give honest decisions....You drunken leaders are like babies! How can you possibly understand or teach the LORD's message? You don't even listen—all you hear is senseless sound after senseless sound" (Isa. 28:7, 9–10, CEV).

PERVERSENESS

Father, Your Word tells me You are "the Rock; [Your] deeds are perfect. Everything [You do] is just and fair. [You are] a faithful God who does no wrong; how just and upright [You are]!" But there are many people who have "acted corruptly toward [You]; when they act so perversely, are they really [Your] children? They are a deceitful and twisted generation" (Deut. 32:4–5, NLT). Father, may everything I do show others that You are my Rock. Cleanse me from all perverseness.

Father, I know that sometimes I will fail You and sin against You. Help me to remember what Your Word says to do when that happens: "When [I] sin against you—for there is no one who does not sin—and you become angry with [me] and give [me] over to the enemy…if [I] have a change of heart…and say, '[I] have sinned, [I] have done wrong, [I] have acted wickedly'; and if [I] turn back to you with all [my] heart and soul…and pray to you…then from heaven, your dwelling place," You will "hear [my] prayer and…forgive all the offenses [I] have committed against you" (1 Kings 8:46–50, NIV). Thank You for forgiving me and showing mercy to me, Lord.

Father, help me to "put away perversity from [my] mouth" and to "keep corrupt talk far from [my] lips" (Prov. 4:24, NIV).

Lord, teach me to seek after integrity, for Your Word tells us, "The integrity of the upright shall guide them, but the willful contrariness and crookedness of the treacherous shall destroy them" (Prov. 11:3, AMP).

Father, protect me from drunkenness and alcoholism and from perversity of any kind. May I be so completely consecrated to Your will for my life that I willingly "do everything without complaining or arguing, so that [I] may become blameless and pure," a child of God "without fault in a crooked and depraved generation," so that I may shine with the light of Your love as I serve You and "hold out the word of life" to those around me (Phil. 2:14–16, NIV).

CHAPTER 6

SPIRITS BRINGING CURSES OF RAPE AND SEXUAL ABUSE

Now as they were making their hearts merry, behold, the men of the city, certain sons of Belial, beset the house round about, and beat at the door, and spake to the master of the house, the old man, saying, Bring forth the man that came into thine house, that we may know him. And the man, the master of the house, went out unto them, Nay, my brethren, nay, I pray you, do not so wickedly; seeing that this man is come into mine house, do not this folly. Behold, here is my daughter a maiden, and his concubine; them I will bring out now, and humble ye them, and do with them what seemeth good unto you: but unto this man do not so vile a thing. But the men would not hearken to him: so the man took his concubine, and brought her forth unto them; and they knew her, and abused her all the night until the morning: and when the day began to spring, they let her go.
—Judges 19:22–25, KJV

THE NEW INTERNATIONAL Version says, "They raped her and abused her throughout the night." This is one of the *vilest* acts recorded in the Word of God. The "sons of Belial" raped the concubine until the next morning. As we continue reading through to the end of the chapter, we find that the concubine actually *died* from this vile act committed against her. She was literally *raped to death.*

> At daybreak the woman went back to the house where her master was staying, fell down at the door and lay there until daylight. When her master got up in the morning and opened the door of the house and stepped out to continue on his way, there lay his concubine, fallen in the doorway of the house, with her hands on the threshold. He said to her, "Get up; let's go." But there was no answer. Then the man put her on his donkey and set out for home.
>
> —Judges 19:26–28, NIV

The Amplified version says, "But there was no answer [for she was dead]." What happens next is very graphic:

> When he reached home, he took a knife and cut up his concubine, limb by limb, into twelve parts and sent them into all the areas of Israel. Everyone who saw it said, "Such a thing has never been seen or done, not since the day the Israelites came up out of Egypt."
>
> —Judges 19:29–30, NIV

The Amplified version says, "There was no such deed done or seen from the day that the Israelites came up out of the land of Egypt to this day." The Contemporary English Version says, "This is horrible! Nothing like this has ever happened since the day Israel left Egypt." The New Living Translation says, "Such a horrible crime has not been committed in all the time since Israel left Egypt."

This abominable act caused civil war in Israel.

> So I took hold of my concubine, cut her in pieces, and sent her throughout all the territory of the inheritance of Israel, because they committed lewdness and outrage in Israel.
>
> —Judges 20:6

The Word of God calls this act "lewdness." Webster defines *lewd* as "evil, wicked, sexually unchaste or licentious, obscene, salacious." The word *obscene* means "disgusting to the senses, repulsive." Thus, Belial causes men to commit vile and obscene acts.

Other spirits working under Belial include rape and sexual abuse. The concubine was raped and abused until she died as a result. The proliferation of rape and sexual abuse, including *incest* and *sodomy*, is the result of the wicked spirit of Belial.

I have ministered to thousands of women and men who were the victims of sexual abuse as children. I also have cast out *spirits of death* that came in during the violation.

When someone is violated in this way, it can be like a death entering that person's soul.

Today, the curse of sexual abuse is rampant in our nation. These filthy spirits are the work of the wicked ruler, Belial.

> So all the men of Israel were gathered against the city, united together as one man. Then the tribes of Israel sent men through all the tribe of Benjamin, saying, "What is this wickedness that has occurred among you? Now therefore, deliver up the men, the perverted men who are in Gibeah, that we may put them to death and remove the evil from Israel!" But the children of Benjamin would not listen to the voice of their brethren, the children of Israel.
>
> —Judges 20:11–13

The tribes of Israel were so repulsed by this act of mass rape that they gathered together against the city of Gibeah and demanded those who were guilty of this act. They decided to put to death the guilty.

There is much controversy today in America concerning the *death penalty*. Many liberals in our nation think it is a cruel method that needs to be outlawed. However, in the Word of God, there were sins that were abominable enough to merit the death penalty. This book is not debating the pros and cons of the death penalty, but suffice it to say that it is found in the Word of God.

The *spirit of Belial* desires for us to tolerate these vile acts in our nation. But there are some sins that are so vile and abominable that they will stir moral indignation in most people, saved or unsaved. The abominable spirits that operate under Belial, inflicting curses upon people, include spirits of rape, incest, molestation, sexual abuse, sexual impurity, uncleanness, filthiness, lasciviousness, sodomy, lewdness, and obscenity.

PRAYERS

ABOMINATIONS

Father, Your Word instructs, "You shall not lie with a male as with a woman. It is an abomination" (Lev. 18:22). Reveal the abominable sin of homosexuality in America, Lord, and bring Your people to repentance.

Lord, Your Word reveals a listing of the abominable sexual perversions that You will judge. Many of these things can be seen in our nation today. They include "anyone who is near of kin to him, to uncover his nakedness." You include the following relatives in this warning: father, mother, father's wife, sister, the daughter of my father, the daughter of my mother, son's daughter, daughter's daughter, father's wife's daughter, father's sister, mother's sister, father's brother, his wife, daughter-in-law, brother's wife, a woman and her daughter, her son's daughter, and her daughter's daughter (Lev. 18:6–19).

Lord, it is Your instruction that a man is not to engage in sexual relations with his neighbor's wife, or a woman with her neighbor's husband (Lev. 18:20).

Father, You give clear instructions that no person is to offer his or her own children as a sacrifice to a false idol or as a sacrifice during a false idolatrous ritual (Lev. 18:21). Father, forgive America for sacrificing millions of unborn children annually on the altar of abortion.

God, it is an abomination to You for a man or woman to mate with any animal. Your Word calls this "perversion" (Lev. 18:23).

Father, You have said that the nation that allows these abominable things to take place is defiled and have promised to cast it away. You will visit iniquity upon it until the land vomits out its inhabitants (Lev. 18:27–28).

God, Your Word declares, "Whoever commits any of these abominations, the persons who commit them shall be cut off from among their people" (Lev. 18:29). God, call America to repentance for its sexual depravity and sin. Redeem Your people and save us.

Lord, these six things You hate; yes, seven are an abomination to You (Prov. 6:16–20):

- A proud look
- A lying tongue
- Hands that shed innocent blood
- A heart that devises wicked plans
- Feet that are swift in running to evil
- A false witness who speaks lies
- One who sows discord among brethren

CROSS-DRESSING

Father, Your Word declares: "Women must not pretend to be men [or wear men's clothing], and men must not pretend to be women [or wear women's clothing]. The LORD your God is disgusted with people who do that" (Deut. 22:5, CEV).

PROSTITUTION

Father, You are "disgusted with men and women who are prostitutes of any kind, and [You] will not accept a gift from them, even if it had been promised" (Deut. 23:18, CEV).

SEXUAL IMPURITY IN THE CHURCH

Father, just as You warned the children of Israel that You would reject and abandon them for allowing sexual impurity and idolatry to take place in the temple, so You are warning America's churches of the evil within. You declare, "The people of Judah have done evil in my eyes, declares the LORD. They have set up their detestable idols in the house that bears my Name and have defiled it" (Jer. 7:30, NIV).

Father, just as in the Bible, the sexual impurity in the churches of America has been exposed and revealed throughout the land. God is saying to America, as He said to Israel, "This is your lot, the portion measured to you from Me, says the Lord, because you have forgotten Me and trusted in falsehood [false gods and alliances with idolatrous nations]. Therefore I Myself will [retaliate], throwing your skirts up over your face, that your shame [of being clad like a slave] may be exposed. I have seen your detestable acts, even your adulteries and your lustful neighings [after idols], and the lewdness of your harlotry on the hills in the field. Woe to you, O Jerusalem! For how long a time yet will you not [meet My conditions and] be made clean?" (Jer. 13:25–27, AMP). Father, call America to repentance, and forgive our land for the rampant sexual immorality, even in Your church.

Father, cause Your people to take heed to Your warning, which states, "But when good people start sinning and doing disgusting things, will they live? No! All their good deeds will be forgotten, and they will be put to death because of their sins" (Ezek. 18:24, cev). May we recognize the danger of allowing impurity to creep into Your church, and may we turn from our wicked ways.

God, You gave Your prophet Ezekiel a hard message, and the truth of Your words must be understood by Your people today, for America has sinned as Israel did. Your warning is strong and fearsome, "God the Master says...you worship no-god idols, you murder at will—and you expect to own this land? You rely on the sword, you engage in obscenities, you indulge in sex at random—anyone, anytime. And you still expect to own this land?...As sure as I am the living God...I'll make this country an empty wasteland....They'll realize that I am God when I devastate the country because of all the obscenities they've practiced" (Ezek. 33:25–29, THE MESSAGE). Father, hear our plea and spare our land!

Father, may we avoid the horrible results of sin that are demonstrated to us through the example of the Romans. Your Word tells us, "Because they exchanged the truth of God for a lie and worshiped and served the creature rather than the Creator...God gave them over and abandoned them to vile affections and degrading passions. For their women exchanged their natural function for an unnatural and abnormal one, and the men also turned from natural relations with women and were set ablaze (burning out, consumed) with lust for one another—men committing shameful acts with men and suffering in their own bodies and personalities the inevitable consequences and penalty of their wrong-doing and going astray, which was [their] fitting retribution. And so, since they did not see fit to acknowledge God or approve of Him or consider Him worth the knowing, God gave them over to a base and condemned mind to do things not proper or decent but loathsome, until they were filled (permeated and saturated) with every kind of unrighteousness" (Rom. 2:25–29, AMP).

Father, cause the people of America to hear Your clear instructions to "kill (deaden, deprive of power) the evil desire lurking in your members [those animal impulses and all that is earthly in you that is employed in sin]: sexual vice, impurity, sensual appetites, unholy desires, and all greed and covetousness, for that is idolatry" (Col. 3:5, AMP). Save our nation, God, and call us to repentance.

Lord, You give us clear advice: "Therefore, get rid of all moral filth and the evil that is so prevalent and humbly accept the word planted in you, which can save you" (James 1:21, NIV). Turn us from our sexual impurity and lust, and let Your Word be firmly planted within our hearts and lives that we may be saved.

CHAPTER 7

CURSED BY PORNOGRAPHY AND PEDOPHILIA

*I will set nothing wicked before my eyes; I hate the
work of those who fall away; it shall not cling to me.*
—Psalm 101:3

THE NEW AMERICAN Standard Bible says, "I will set
no worthless thing before my eyes." This shows us the
attitude and abhorrence we, as people of God, should have
toward anything related to Belial. We should resist and
abhor anything base, vile, unworthy, unclean, ungodly,
contemptible, wicked, blasphemous, or shameful.

We are to abhor that which is evil and cleave to that
which is good. *Abhor* is a strong word. It means "to regard
with extreme repugnance, to loathe; to turn aside or keep
away from, especially in scorn or shuddering fear, to
reject, to hate."

This verse can apply to the present-day rise of pornography and the sexual filth that Belial is flooding our nation

with. One of the vilest forms of pornography is "kiddie porn," which is a thriving business supported by pedophiles. *Pedophilia* is sexual perversion in which children are the preferred sexual objects.

Most states have obscenity laws that are being challenged by those who feel as if government should provide no constraint. *Obscenity* is defined as "the state of being obscene." *Obscene* means "disgusting to the senses, repulsive, abhorrent to morality or virtue."

Pornography opens the door for a host of evil spirits of lust and perversion. There has also been a connection between pornography and rape in some studies. I believe Belial is a ruling spirit over spirits of pornography, whoredom, prostitution, and other sexual spirits.

Sexual impurity is another strong spirit that is under Belial's control, including spirits of homosexuality and lesbianism (perversion). If this spirit can pervert the morals of a nation through sexual immorality, he can bring the judgment and curse of the Lord upon a nation.

PRAYERS

Lord, Your Word describes the actions of a child molester as "a wicked man" who "hunts down the weak, who are caught in the schemes he devises." You describe this wicked person who "lies in wait near the villages...watching in secret for his victims. He lies in wait like a lion in cover; he lies in wait to catch the helpless; he catches the helpless and drags them off in his net. His victims are crushed, they collapse; they fall under his strength" (Ps. 10:2, 8–10, NIV). Protect the children of this nation from such wickedness, Lord, and bring Your judgment down upon these wicked predators.

Father, our nation is filled with the impurities and perverseness of men and women who do only what is "right in [their] own eyes" (Judg. 17:6). Reveal Your righteousness to America, Lord, and cause us to "lift up [our] eyes to the hills," for our "help comes from the LORD, the Maker of heaven and earth" (Ps. 121:1–3, NIV).

Father, Your Word tells us that wickedness begins in our eyes. It is when we take our eyes off You and place them on worldly things that we are enticed and drawn away by our sinful lust (James 1:14).

THE PROGRESSION OF PORNOGRAPHY

Father, pornography is an insidious evil that begins with a first glance at someone immodestly dressed, and "we are tempted by our own desires that drag us off and trap us. Our desires make us sin, and when sin is finished with us, it leaves us dead" (James 1:14–15, CEV).

Lord, when we yield to the temptation to our eyes, those sinful activities become an addiction to us, and we become "a slave of sin" (John 8:34). When pornography has trapped a person, that person becomes a "slave of depravity—for a man is a slave to whatever has mastered him" (2 Pet. 2:19, NIV).

Lord, cause Americans who are addicted to the sinful allure of pornography to understand that Your Word teaches, "Can you build a fire in your lap and not burn your pants? Can you walk barefoot on hot coals and not get blisters?" (Prov. 6:27–28, THE MESSAGE). Reveal the burns of pornography upon the souls of Americans, and turn us away from its wicked entrapments.

Father, remove the stain of pornography from Your church. Help us to hear the cry of Peter, who warns, "I implore you as aliens and strangers and exiles [in this world] to abstain from the sensual urges (the evil desires, the passions of the flesh, your lower nature) that wage war against the soul" (1 Pet. 2:11, AMP).

Lord, keep us from believing that a little bit of sin— a little bit of pornography—won't hurt us. If we do not turn away from this sin, You will tell us plainly: "I never knew you. Away from me, you evildoers!" (Matt. 7:23, NIV).

Father, all the evils of sexual impurity—including pornography—make us "unclean" in Your sight. "For from within, out of men's hearts, come evil thoughts, sexual immorality, theft, murder, adultery, greed, malice, deceit, lewdness, envy, slander, arrogance and folly. All these evils come from inside and make a man 'unclean'" (Mark 7:20–23, NIV).

Lord, the sins of sexual impurity will separate us from You and cause You to hide Your face from us and refuse to hear us when we call (Isa. 59:2).

Father, ultimately, if we continue to cling to pornographic images and thoughts, we will even be denied entrance into heaven. "Those who practice such things will not inherit the kingdom of God" (Gal. 5:21).

God, because pornography can become an addiction that is hard to get free of, we must actively seek after Your Word and You to break its hold upon us. You tell us to, "Be on your guard and stay awake. Your enemy, the devil, is like a roaring lion, sneaking around to find someone to attack" (1 Pet. 5:8, CEV).

Father, You tell us in Your Word that we can keep our lives pure "by living according to your word." Help us to make this commitment: "I seek you with all my heart; do not let me stray from your commands. I have hidden your word in my heart that I might not sin against you" (Ps. 119:9–11, NIV).

Lord, there is one guaranteed way for me to live free of sexual impurity and the temptation of pornographic sin. Paul told us how to avoid sin when he said, "All I want is to know Christ and the power that raised him to life....I have not yet reached my goal, and I am not perfect. But Christ has taken hold of me....I don't feel that I have already arrived. But I forget what is behind, and I struggle for what is ahead. I run toward the goal, so that I can win the prize of being called to heaven. This is the prize that God offers because of what Christ Jesus has done. All of us who are mature should think in this same way....We must keep going in the direction that we are now headed" (Phil. 3:10–16, CEV).

Father, how I thank You for this promise: "For no temptation (no trial regarded as enticing to sin), [no matter how it comes or where it leads] has overtaken you and laid hold on you that is not common to man [that is, no temptation or trial has come to you that is beyond human resistance and that is not adjusted and adapted and belonging to human experience, and such as man can bear]. But God is faithful [to His Word and to His compassionate nature], and He [can be trusted] not to let you be tempted and tried and assayed beyond your ability and strength of resistance and power to endure, but with the temptation He will [always] also provide the way out (the means of escape to a landing place), that you may be capable and strong and powerful to bear up under it patiently" (1 Cor. 10:13, AMP).

Lord, one of the greatest promises in Your Word is this: "My power is strongest when you are weak" (2 Cor. 12:9, CEV). With Your power, we can live free of the snare of pornography.

CHILD MOLESTATION AND PEDOPHILIA

Father, Your Word tells the horrible story of Amnon's brutal rape of his half sister, Tamar (2 Sam. 13:1–22). By that terrible sin, he became a pedophile, and he destroyed the life of Tamar and created hatred and animosity in King David's family that caused rejection, murder, and devastation. Father, wake America up to the devastation that this abhorrent sin of pedophilia and child molestation has caused. Call us to repentance, and bring down Your judgment on those who will not turn from their wicked ways.

Father, You said that if anyone hurts one of Your little children, "it would be better for him if a millstone were hung around his neck, and he were drowned in the depth of the sea" (Matt. 18:6). Millions of Your little children have been devastated by the sin of molestation. We cry out to You for mercy and restoration for each one of them, and we pledge our lives to doing all we can to purge America of its pedophiles.

Father, in the strongest possible words, You warn us of the dangers of sin by saying, "If your hand or foot causes you to sin, cut it off and cast it from you. It is better for you to enter into life lame or maimed, rather than having two hands or two feet, to be cast into the everlasting fire. And if your eye causes you to sin, pluck it out and cast it from you. It is better for you to enter into life with one eye, rather than having two eyes, to be cast into hell fire" (Matt. 18:8–9). You gave this warning in the context of warning those who hurt little children. Help us to understand the depth of Your love for children and to do everything we can to protect them in America.

CHILDREN ARE GOD'S BEST GIFTS

Teach us to value children the way You do, Lord. You have said, "Don't you see that children are GOD's best gift? The fruit of the womb his generous legacy? Like a warrior's fistful of arrows are the children of a vigorous youth. Oh, how blessed are you parents, with your quivers full of children! Your enemies don't stand a chance against you; you'll sweep them right off your doorstep" (Ps. 127:3–5, THE MESSAGE).

Father, You demonstrated Your love for children when the people crowded around You with their babies in the hope that You would bless them. When the disciples saw this, they tried to shoo off the parents. But You called them back and said, "Let these children alone. Don't get between them and me. These children are the kingdom's pride and joy. Mark this: Unless you accept God's kingdom in the simplicity of a child, you'll never get in" (Luke 18:16–17, THE MESSAGE). Teach me to live for You in the simplicity of childhood and to protect Your children from harm.

CHAPTER 8

CURSED WITH LAWLESSNESS AND REBELLION

*From you comes forth one who plots evil
against the LORD, a wicked counselor.*
—Nahum 1:11

T HE NEW JERUSALEM Bible says, "From you has emerged someone plotting evil against Yahweh, one of Belial's counsellors." Nahum is prophesying judgment against Nineveh and the Assyrian Empire. The king of Assyria was actually plotting against the Lord. One translation says, "Who is this king of yours who dares to plot against the Lord?"

This is the spirit of *antichrist.* Psalm 2:2–3 says: "The kings of the earth set themselves, and the rulers take counsel together, against the LORD and against His Anointed, saying, 'Let us break Their bonds in pieces and cast away Their cords from us.'"

There you have it; the ultimate goal of Belial is to *cast*

off restraint. The church is a restraining force in the earth against the filth and ungodliness Belial desires to flood upon the earth.

The Amplified Bible says, "...and cast Their cords [of control] from us." These "kings of the earth" are the spirits of *lawlessness* and *rebellion*. While there is no law, people run wild.

America's entire judicial system was founded on the Judeo-Christian ethic found in the Bible. In other words, the Bible is the foundation of our legal system. A society that rejects the Bible as its moral authority will eventually have problems with its judicial system. Belial hates the restraining power of the Bible, the Holy Spirit, and the church. This is why he attacks them so viciously.

Belial desires immorality and ungodliness to reign without any restraint. Belial is responsible for an attack upon our judicial system that we are experiencing today in America. Laws against homosexuality, lesbianism, and adultery, which were once a part of our legal code, are now being removed.

Homosexuals believe they have a right to live ungodly lifestyles. Many are clamoring, "Leave me alone, and let me do what I want. I don't want any preacher to tell me what is right and wrong." Others are asserting, "Give us separation of church and state. Take prayer out of the schools." This is all an attempt to cast off restraint.

PRAYERS

RESTRAINT

Father, the faithful and godly minority in America has begun to feel as Job felt when he was being persecuted and mocked. His words describe our feelings, for he cried out, "Sons of the worthless and nameless...I am a byword to them. They abhor me, they stand aloof from me, and do not refrain from spitting in my face or at the sight of me...they have cast off the bridle [of restraint] before me. On my right hand rises the rabble brood; they jostle me and push away my feet, and they cast up against me their ways of destruction [like an advancing army]" (Job 30:8–12, AMP). Father, rescue us as You did Job, and restore restraint and godliness to America.

Lord, Your Word has clearly identified the reason America is falling into godlessness and immorality. You tell us clearly, "Where there is no revelation ("no vision [no redemptive revelation of God]," AMP), the people cast off restraint" (Prov. 29:18). This nation has forsaken the restraints of Your Word for their own godless, liberal agendas. Have mercy on America, Lord, and reestablish us in Your laws.

Father, Your Word tells us what happened when Your people in Israel abandoned Your ways: "God indicts the whole population: 'No one is faithful. No one loves. No one knows the first thing about God. All this cussing and lying and killing, theft and loose sex, sheer anarchy, one murder after another! And because of all this, the very land itself weeps and everything in it is grief-stricken" (Hosea 4:1–3, THE MESSAGE). And You told the priests and prophets: "But don't look for someone to blame. No finger pointing!...Because you've turned your back on knowledge, I've turned my back on you priests. Because you refuse to recognize the revelation of God, I'm no longer recognizing your children" (vv. 4–10). This sounds like America today, Father. Forgive Your Christian leaders for turning our backs on Your revelation, and redeem Your church so we can lead America into righteousness.

REBELLION

Father, Your Word reveals Moses's disappointment with the Levites—Israel's spiritual leaders. When he was about to die, he called the Levites together, and he told them, "This is The Book of God's Law. Keep it beside the sacred chest that holds the agreement the LORD your God made with Israel. This book is proof that you know what the LORD wants you to do. I know how stubborn and rebellious you and the rest of the Israelites are. You have rebelled against the LORD while I have been alive, and it will only get worse after I am gone. So call together the leaders and officials of the tribes of Israel. I will bring this book and read every word of it to you, and I will call the sky and the earth as witnesses that all of you know what you are supposed to do. I am going to die soon, and I know that in the future you will stop caring about what is right and what is wrong, and so you will disobey the LORD and stop living the way I told you to live. The LORD will be angry, and terrible things will happen to you" (Deut. 31:26–29, CEV). His words describe a great host of America's spiritual leaders, Lord. Help me to continue to serve You with a godly and righteous heart, and keep me from failing You as others have.

Father, when Saul became so proud and arrogant that he disobeyed You, You sent Samuel to tell him, "Does the LORD really want sacrifices and offerings? No! He doesn't want your sacrifices. He wants you to obey him. Rebelling against God or disobeying him because you are proud is just as bad as worshiping idols or asking them for advice. You refused to do what God told you, so God has decided that you can't be king" (1 Sam. 15:22–23, CEV). Keep me from becoming rebellious, proud, and disobedient to You, Father. May You never have to say about me, "I'm sorry that I gave you your ministry, because in your pride you failed to obey Me."

Father, after the children of Israel had wandered in the wilderness for forty years, You confronted them about their rebelliousness, and You told them, "Understand that the LORD your God is not giving you this good land to possess because of your righteousness, for you are a stiff-necked people. Remember! Do not forget how you provoked the LORD your God to wrath in the wilderness. From the day that you departed from the land of Egypt until you came to this place, you have been rebellious against the LORD" (Deut. 9:6–7). Just as Moses pleaded with You to have mercy on the people and not destroy them, so I plead with You, Father, to forgive America for its rebelliousness and sin, and I ask You to save our nation from destruction.

Lord, You place a high priority upon obedience. You are a "Father of orphans" and a "champion of widows." You make "homes for the homeless" and lead "prisoners to freedom." But You "leave rebels to rot in hell" (Ps. 68:6, THE MESSAGE).

Father, over and over in Your Word You extended mercy and grace to the rebellious Israelites. When they turned back to You, You forgave them and restored them to Your favor. You told them, "In returning and rest you shall be saved; in quietness and confidence shall be your strength" (Isa. 30:15). You waited for them to return to You so that You could show them Your grace and mercy, for You are a God of justice (v. 18). Father, we plead for You to be patient and wait for America to turn back to

You. Show us Your grace and mercy, Father, that we may return in obedience to serving You.

EVIL IMAGINATIONS

Lord, Paul gave a warning about those who turn away from You: "Yes, they knew God, but they wouldn't worship him as God or even give him thanks. And they began to think up foolish ideas of what God was like. As a result, their minds became dark and confused. Claiming to be wise, they instead became utter fools" (Rom. 1:21–22, NLT). So many people in our world today have made up foolish ideas about You, and as a result have minds that have become dark and confused. They profess to be part of a "new age," but they look like fools. Lord, raise up a godly army that will keep these fools from confusing and pulling others away from You. Move by Your Holy Spirit to destroy the influence of those who claim to know more than You.

Lord, make us into a strong, bold spiritual army in America. "We are human, but we don't wage war as humans do. We use God's mighty weapons, not worldly weapons, to knock down the strongholds of human reasoning and to destroy false arguments. We destroy every proud obstacle that keeps people from knowing God. We capture their rebellious thoughts and teach them to obey Christ" (2 Cor. 10:3–5, NLT).

EVIL

Lord, "You are not a God who takes pleasure in evil," and "the wicked cannot dwell" with You. "The arrogant cannot stand in your presence," and "you hate all who do wrong" (Ps. 5:4–5, NIV).

Lord, You have instructed Your followers to "depart from evil and do good; seek peace and pursue it" (Ps. 34:14). I have committed my life to following Your instructions, Lord.

Father, You have told Your followers, "Don't worry about the wicked or envy those who do wrong. For like grass, they soon fade away. Like spring flowers, they soon wither" (Ps. 37:1–2, NLT).

Father, I will be still in Your presence and wait patiently for You to act. I will not worry about evil people who prosper, and I will not fret about their wicked schemes (Ps. 37: 7).

Father, I am so thankful for Your Word, which promises, "It is better to be godly and have little than to be evil and rich. For the strength of the wicked will be shattered, but the LORD takes care of the godly. Day by day the LORD takes care of the innocent, and they will receive an inheritance that lasts forever. They will not be disgraced in hard times; even in famine they will have more than enough. But the wicked will die. The LORD's enemies are like flowers in a field—they will disappear like smoke" (Ps. 37:16–20, NLT).

Father, I will obey Your Word to "turn from evil and do good, and you will live in the land forever. For the LORD loves justice, and he will never abandon the godly" (Ps. 37:27–28, NLT).

Lord, "The wicked wait in ambush for the godly, looking for an excuse to kill them. But the LORD will not let the wicked succeed or let the godly be condemned when they are put on trial" (Ps. 37:32–33, NLT).

Father, just like the psalmist David, I see the evil in our land, and I know that You will cause the plans of evildoers to fail. Like David, I say to the evildoers, "You people may be strong and brag about your sins, but God can be trusted day after day. You plan brutal crimes, and your lying words cut like a sharp razor. You would rather do evil than good, and tell lies than speak the truth. You love to say cruel things, and your words are a trap. God will destroy you forever! He will grab you and drag you from your homes. You will be uprooted and left to die. When good people see this fearsome sight, they will laugh and say, 'Just look at them now! Instead of trusting God, they trusted their wealth and their cruelty'" (Ps. 52:1–7, CEV).

Lord, at times it seems like the evil plans and schemes of men and women who are living godless lives will succeed and Your children will suffer because of them. But I am committing myself to taking a stand on Your Word. I stand in agreement with Psalm 91, and I will:

1. Live under Your protection and stay in Your shadow

2. Proclaim that You are my fortress and place of safety

3. Believe You are my God and trust You

4. Trust that You will keep me safe from secret traps and deadly diseases

5. Be safe and secure under Your wings

6. Have no fear of dangers at night or in the daytime, because Your faithfulness is like a shield and a city wall

7. Have faith that no disease will strike in the night and no disasters will come in the daytime

8. Know that though thousands fall to danger around me, I will not be harmed

9. See You punish the wicked with my own eyes, and I will run to You for safety

10. Experience no terrible disasters striking my home, my family, or me

11. Believe that You have commanded Your angels to protect me wherever I go

12. Declare that Your power will be stronger than the strongest lions or the most deadly snakes

13. Be safe because I love You and serve You

14. Call on You when I am in trouble, and You will protect and honor me

15. Live a long life and live to see Your saving power

Father, sometimes unjust leaders boldly claim that God is on their side, yet they are leaders who permit injustice. They gang up on the righteous and condemn the innocent to death through their unjust laws and regulations. But when this happens, You are my fortress and the mighty rock on which I stand. You have promised to turn their sins back upon them and destroy them in the way they planned to destroy Your children (Ps. 94:20–23).

Father, in this day when it seems that godless men and godless laws are destroying the godly life and foundations on which this nation was founded, Your Word brings courage and strength to Your people. In it You have promised that our "children will be successful everywhere," and "an entire generation of godly people will be blessed." Your people will possess wealth, and our good deeds will last forever. "Light shines in the darkness for the godly." Your people will be "generous, compassionate, and righteous." Good will come to those who lend money generously and conduct business fairly. We will not be overcome by evil. As we confidently trust in You to care for us, we will be confident and fearless and face our foes triumphantly. We will have influence and honor, and when the wicked see this, it will infuriate them. They will grind their teeth in anger and slink away as their hopes are thwarted (Ps. 112, NLT).

Father, You have promised, "Whoever listens to me will dwell safely, and will be secure, without fear of evil" (Prov. 1:33).

Father, You have warned Your children, "Do not enter the path of the wicked, and do not walk in the way of evil" (Prov. 4:14).

Father, You have counseled Your children, "Do not turn to the right or the left; remove your foot from evil" (Prov. 4:27).

Father, Your Word promises, "No grave trouble will overtake the righteous, but the wicked shall be filled with evil" (Prov. 12:21).

Father, "a wise man fears and departs from evil, but a fool rages and is self-confident" (Prov. 14:16).

Father, help me to carefully consider what I say and to be sure my answers are godly and truthful. You have said, "The heart of the righteous studies how to answer, but the mouth of the wicked pours forth evil" (Prov. 15:28).

PRAYER AGAINST EVIL

"O Lord, rescue me from evil people. Protect me from those who are violent, those who plot evil in their hearts and stir up trouble all day long. Their tongues sting like a snake; the venom of a viper drips from their lips. O Lord, keep me out of the hands of the wicked. Protect me from those who are violent, for they are plotting against me. The proud have set a trap to catch me; they have stretched out a net; they have placed traps all along the way. I said to the Lord, 'You are my God!' Listen, O Lord, to my cries for mercy! O Sovereign Lord, the strong one who rescued me, you protected me on the day of battle. Lord, do not let evil people have their way. Do not let their evil schemes succeed, or they will become proud. Let my enemies be destroyed by the very evil they have planned for me. Let burning coals fall down on their heads. Let them be thrown into the fire or into watery pits from which they can't escape. Don't let liars prosper here in our land. Cause great disasters to fall on the violent. But I know the Lord will help those they persecute; he will give justice to the poor. Surely righteous people are praising your name; the godly will live in your presence" (Ps. 140, NLT).

CHAPTER 9

THE CURSE OF UNGODLY SOUL TIES AND GODLESSNESS

Do not be unequally yoked together with unbe-
lievers. For what fellowship has righteousness with
lawlessness? And what communion has light with
darkness? And what accord has Christ with Belial?
Or what part has a believer with an unbeliever?
—2 Corinthians 6:14–15

WHEN THERE IS an unequal yoke between believers and unbelievers, we call this an *ungodly soul tie*. Breaking ungodly soul ties is a key to deliverance. Ungodly association causes evil spirits to be transferred. If Belial cannot directly control you, he will influence you through ungodly association.

Associating with the wrong people can cause you to receive an *evil transfer* of spirits. One of the keys to being delivered from Belial's control is to break every ungodly soul tie and to obey the Word of God, which says, "Do not be unequally yoked together with unbelievers" (2 Cor. 6:14). The Amplified Bible says, "Do not be unequally yoked with unbelievers [do not make mismated alliances with them or come under a different yoke with them, inconsistent with your faith]."

This is the only time the name Belial is mentioned in the New Testament. I believe the Spirit of God chose this word to bring revelation to a spirit that the church *must not in any way* be in fellowship with.

Verse 15 ties Belial with unrighteousness, darkness, infidels, and idolatry. The first reference to Belial in the Word of God ties him to *idolatry*. The Corinthians had been saved from a lifestyle of idolatry.

As stated before, I believe that Belial is an End Time spirit who will be an enemy of the church. We are to separate ourselves from all uncleanness and filthiness that is associated with this ruling spirit.

The church at Corinth also had a problem with carnality. There were strife, envy, contention, sexual impurity, and even drunkenness taking place within the church. The apostle Paul wrote the letter to Corinth to correct these problems and to set things in order.

A Flood of Ungodliness

When the waves of death surrounded me, the floods of ungodliness made me afraid.

—2 Samuel 22:5

The literal translation of this verse is "…the floods of Belial." This verse is a portion of a song David sang in the day the Lord delivered him out of the hand of all his enemies and out of the hand of Saul.

The American Standard Version says, "The floods of ungodliness made me afraid." Belial has released a flood of ungodliness upon our nation. *Ungodly* is defined as "denying God or being disobedient to Him: impious, irreligious, contrary to moral law, sinful, wicked."

Belial is responsible for the flood of ungodliness manifested through Hollywood, television, and the mass media. Belial is responsible for rebellion and disobedience to God. This spirit has cursed many, causing them to be irreligious and impious.

Having no reverence—no fear of God—is the result of Belial's influence. To *flood* means "to cover, to inundate, to fill abundantly or excessively." Belial desires to cover the earth with filth and immorality. This flood also includes the persecution that comes against the Lord's anointed, David.

Belial desires to murder and destroy the Lord's anointed. He is a strongman who attacks ministers and churches. The New American Standard Bible says, "The torrents of destruction overwhelmed me." We find that the word *torrent* is defined as "an outpouring, a rush."

Perdition means "destruction." Spirits of *death and destruction* work with Belial to assail the servants of God. We have already seen that Jezebel works under Belial to destroy true servants of God. Lies, slander, seduction, lust, and pride are all weapons used against the Lord's anointed.

It is important to intercede against Belial's curses. When the enemy shall come in like a flood, the Spirit of the Lord will lift up a standard against him. The Lord will lift up a standard against the floods of Belial. The prayers and intercessions of God's people will be a standard against this flood.

COMING AGAINST BELIAL

> But the sons of Belial shall be all of them as thorns thrust away, because they cannot be taken with hands: but the man that shall touch them must be fenced with iron and the staff of a spear; and they shall be utterly burned with fire in the same place.
>
> —2 Samuel 23:6–7, KJV

This verse compares the "sons of Belial" to thorns that cannot be handled. Those who deal with Belial "must be fenced with iron and the staff of a spear." A *thorn* is something that causes distress or irritation. To be *thorny* means to be full of difficulties or controversial points.

This verse pronounces the judgment upon Belial and those who follow him: "They shall be utterly burned with fire in the same place." This is a reference to eternal damnation in hellfire. I believe that Belial is a spirit that will cause many to die lost and spend eternity in hell.

"Fenced with iron and the staff of a spear" is a reference

to putting on the whole armor of God. We cannot deal with this spirit without the whole armor of God.

The Lord is raising up intercessors and preachers to come against this spirit in the last days. This is an End Time spirit assigned to corrupt the earth, but the Lord has an *End Time people* to combat him. The Young Literal Translation says, "And the man who cometh against them...."

David had to fight and overcome the men controlled by Belial. David is a type of the New Testament church. He is a type of the prophetic church the Lord is raising up in this hour. Just as David overcame, we will also overcome this End Time spirit.

We will not handle this spirit with our natural hands. He is too thorny and difficult for that. But we must and will attack him in the power of the Spirit, wearing the whole armor of God.

PRAYERS

SEPARATION FROM BELIAL

Father, You have instructed us, "Do not be unequally yoked together with unbelievers. For what fellowship has righteousness with lawlessness? And what communion has light with darkness? And what accord has Christ with Belial? Or what part has a believer with an unbeliever? And what agreement has the temple of God with idols? For you are the temple of the living God.... Therefore come out from among them and be separate.... Do not touch what is unclean, and I will receive you" (2 Cor. 6:14–17).

Father, You have stressed how important it is to guard our hearts from evil by saying, "Keep and guard your heart with all vigilance and above all that you guard, for out of it flow the springs of life" (Prov. 4:23, AMP).

Father, help us to remember Your Word: "God's will is for you to be holy, so stay away from all sexual sin. Then each of you will control his own body and live in holiness and honor—not in lustful passion like the pagans who do not know God and his ways.... God has called us to live holy lives, not impure lives" (1 Thess. 4:3–5, 7, NLT).

Father, help us to remember to guard our souls by refusing to be united to anything that is evil, for Your Word tells us, "Beloved, I implore you as aliens and strangers and exiles [in this world] to abstain from the sensual urges (the evil desires, the passions of the flesh, your lower nature) that wage war against the soul" (1 Pet. 2:11, AMP).

GUARD YOUR SOUL

Father, I have committed myself to: "Love the LORD your God with all your heart and with all your soul and with all your strength" (Deut. 6:5, NIV).

Lord, it is for my own good that You have asked me to love You with all my heart *and all my soul*. For You have said, "What does the LORD your God ask of you but to fear the LORD your God, to walk in all his ways, to love him, to serve the LORD your God with all your heart and with all your soul, and to observe the LORD's commands and decrees that I am giving you today for your own good?" (Deut. 10:12–13, NIV).

Father, Your Word warns us of the dangers that can come because of deep soul ties. You have said, "If your brother, the son of your mother, your son or your daughter, the wife of your bosom, or your friend *who is as your own soul*, secretly entices you, saying, 'Let us go and serve other gods,' which you have not known…you shall not consent to him or listen to him, nor shall your eye pity him, nor shall you spare him or conceal him; but you shall surely kill him; your hand shall be first against him to put him to death, and afterward the hand of all the people. And you shall stone him with stones until he dies, because he sought to entice you away from the LORD your God, who brought you out of the land of Egypt, from the house of bondage" (Deut. 13:6, 8–10, emphasis added).

Lord, You have told me, "Now devote your heart and soul to seeking the LORD your God" (1 Chron. 22:19, NIV). May I always remember that if I allow my soul to be unguarded and develop a deep soul tie with an unbeliever, it could separate me from You.

Father, You warn us that our soul can be trapped by anger, and You say, "Make no friendship with an angry man, and with a furious man do not go, lest you learn his ways and set a snare for your soul" (Prov. 22:24–25). Keep me from binding my soul to anger.

Father, we live in a world where many have lost their hope because of desperate situations and rampant godlessness. Yet Your Word promises how our souls can be constantly filled with hope for the future. You tell us in Your Word, "Eat honey, my son, for it is good; honey from the comb is sweet to your taste. Know also that wisdom is sweet to your soul; if you find it, there is a future hope for you, and your hope will not be cut off" (Prov. 24:13–14, NIV).

Father, teach me to remember that my soul must be filled with Your goodness—not with things of this world. You have told us, "Why spend money on what is not bread, and your labor on what does not satisfy? Listen, listen to me, and eat what is good, and your soul will delight in the richest of fare" (Prov. 55:2, NIV).

Father, when we find that our hearts and souls are weary and bound by cares and unhealthy soul ties, then we must "stand in the ways and see, and ask for the old paths, where the good way is, and walk in it; then you will find rest for your souls" (Jer. 6:16).

Lord, teach me to respect the spiritual leaders You have placed over me, as You have instructed in Your Word: "Obey those who rule over you, and be submissive, for they watch out for your souls, as those who must give account. Let them do so with joy and not with grief, for that would be unprofitable for you" (Heb. 13:17).

UNGODLINESS

Lord, Your servant David came to a time in his life when he felt as though he was drowning in a flood of enemies who were trying to destroy him, yet You rescued him. I pray that You will rescue me from the floodwaters of trouble, and I too will praise You as David praised You. "Our LORD and our God, you are my mighty rock, my fortress, my protector. You are the rock where I am safe. You are my shield, my powerful weapon, and my place of shelter. You rescue me and keep me from being hurt. I praise you, our Lord! I prayed to you, and you rescued me from my enemies. Death, like ocean waves, surrounded me, and I was almost swallowed by its flooding waters. Ropes from the world of the dead had coiled around me, and death had set a trap in my path. I was in terrible trouble when I called out to you, but from your temple you heard me and answered my prayer.... You roared at the sea, and its deepest channels.... You reached down from heaven, and you lifted me from deep in the ocean. You rescued me from enemies who were hateful and too powerful for me.... Only you are a mighty rock" (2 Sam. 22:1–7, 16–18, 32, CEV). You are my strong fortress, and You set me free.

Father, when the flood of sin and ungodliness threatens my life and my family, I will call upon You as David did and proclaim, "The voice of the Lord echoes over the oceans. The glorious Lord God thunders above the roar of the raging sea, and his voice is mighty and marvelous.... The Lord rules on his throne, king of the flood forever. Pray that our Lord will make us strong and give us peace" (Ps. 29:3–4, 10–11, CEV).

"Save me, God! I am about to drown. I am sinking deep in the mud, and my feet are slipping. I am about to be swept under by a mighty flood.... But

I pray to you, LORD. So when the time is right, answer me and help me with your wonderful love. Don't let me sink in the mud, but save me from my enemies and from the deep water. Don't let me be swept away by a flood or drowned in the ocean or swallowed by death. Answer me, LORD! You are kind and good" (Ps. 69:1–2, 13–16, CEV).

Father, I am not afraid of the flood of unrighteousness and ungodliness that is rising in our nation. I know that You will save Your people, just as You promise in Your Word: "By your power you made a path through the sea, and you smashed the heads of sea monsters. You crushed the heads of the monster Leviathan, then fed him to wild creatures in the desert. You opened the ground for streams and springs and dried up mighty rivers. You rule the day and the night, and you put the moon and the sun in place.... Violent enemies are hiding in every dark corner of the earth. Don't disappoint those in need or make them turn from you, but help the poor and homeless to shout your praises" (Ps. 74:13–16, 20–21, CEV).

Father, I will not fear the flood of ungodliness in our nation, for Your Word promises, "Now the LORD will get furious and do to his enemies, both near and far, what they did to his people. He will attack like a flood in a mighty windstorm. Nations in the west and the east will then honor and praise his wonderful name" (Isa. 59:18–19, CEV).

Lord, the day will come when You will come in a flood of godliness and power, and all the flood-waters of sin and ungodliness will give way to the fresh floods of glory and power from You. Your Word prophesies, "And it will come to pass in that day that the mountains shall drip with new wine, the hills shall flow with milk, and all the brooks of Judah shall be flooded with water; a fountain shall flow from the house of the LORD and water the Valley of Acacias.... For the LORD dwells in Zion" (Joel 3:18, 21).

Lord, I want my life to be built upon the strong rock of Jesus Christ, for then when the flood of ungodliness sweeps in, I will be like the wise man who built his house on the rock: "And the rain descended, the floods came, and the winds blew and beat on that house; and it did not fall, for it was founded on the rock" (Matt. 7:25).

AVOIDING UNGODLINESS

Father, You give us the steps to follow to avoid being snared by ungodliness: "Be diligent to present your-self approved to God, a worker who does not need to be ashamed, rightly dividing the word of truth.

But shun profane and idle babblings, for they will increase to more ungodliness" (2 Tim. 2:15–16).

Lord, help me to follow the advice that the apostle Paul gave his young helper Timothy: "You therefore, my son, be strong in the grace that is in Christ Jesus. And the things that you have heard from me among many witnesses, commit these to faithful men who will be able to teach others also. You therefore must endure hardship as a good soldier of Jesus Christ. No one engaged in warfare entangles himself with the affairs of this life, that he may please him who enlisted him as a soldier" (2 Tim. 2:1–4).

Father, the apostle Paul listed the steps that You have taken to ensure that Your followers do not fall into ungodliness. I praise You for these blessings (Eph. 1:3–14):

1. Blessed be the God and Father of our Lord Jesus Christ, who has blessed us with every spiritual blessing in the heavenly places in Christ.

2. He chose us in Him before the foundation of the world, that we should be holy and without blame before Him in love.

3. He predestined us to adoption as sons by Jesus Christ to Himself, according to the good pleasure of His will.

4. He made us accepted in the Beloved.

5. In Him we have redemption through His blood,

the forgiveness of sins, according to the riches of His grace, which He made to abound toward us in all wisdom and prudence.

6. He made known to us the mystery of His will, according to His good pleasure, which He purposed in Himself.

7. In Him also we have obtained an inheritance, being predestined according to the purpose of Him who works all things according to the counsel of His will.

8. In Him you also trusted, after you heard the word of truth, the gospel of your salvation; in whom also, having believed, you were sealed with the Holy Spirit of promise.

9. He is the guarantee of our inheritance until the redemption of the purchased possession, to the praise of His glory.

Father, just as Paul prayed for the believers at Philippi, I pray for my fellow believers that we may not fall into ungodliness. "I thank my God upon every remembrance of you, always in every prayer of mine making request for you all with joy, for your fellowship in the gospel from the first day until now, being confident of this very thing, that He who has begun a good work in you will complete it until the day of Jesus Christ.... And this I pray, that your love may abound still more and more in knowledge and all discernment, that you may approve the things that are excellent, that you may be sincere and without offense till the day of Christ, being filled with the fruits of righteousness which are by Jesus Christ, to the glory and praise of God" (Phil. 1:3–6, 9–11).

Lord, "blessed is the man who walks not in the counsel of the ungodly, nor stands in the path of sinners, nor sits in the seat of the scornful; but his delight is in the law of the LORD, and in His law he meditates day and night. He shall be like a tree planted by the rivers of water, that brings forth its fruit in its season, whose leaf also shall not wither; and whatever he does shall prosper" (Ps. 1:1–3).

CHAPTER 10

WICKED PLOTS AGAINST THE GODLY

*An ungodly man digs up evil, and it is
on his lips like a burning fire.*
—Proverbs 16:27

THE AMERICAN STANDARD Version says, "A worthless man deviseth mischief." The Contemporary English Version says, "Worthless people plan trouble." To *devise* means "to plan to bring about." A *plot* is a secret plan usually for accomplishing an evil or unlawful end.

Belial causes men to plan and plot evil. Psalm 37:12 says, "The wicked plots against the just." There are people involved in forms of witchcraft that are planning to destroy the church. We have heard reports of witches fasting to break up marriages of Christian leaders and to disrupt the church.

It is almost hard to believe that there are actually people this wicked. I believe it because the Word of God states it.

Most people would be shocked to know the types of gross sins and plots taking place behind closed doors.

Psalm 37:32 says, "The wicked watches the righteous, and seeks to slay him." The Amplified version says, "The wicked lie in wait for the [uncompromisingly] righteous and seek to put them to death." The New Living Translation says, "The wicked wait in ambush for the godly, looking for an excuse to kill them."

What a sobering thought! No wonder the Word of God admonishes us to be *sober and vigilant*. Belial will influence men to plot against the righteous.

CURSING THE LORD'S ANOINTED

And when king David came to Bahurim, behold, thence came out a man of the family of the house of Saul, whose name was Shimei, the son of Gera: he came forth, and cursed still as he came. And he cast stones at David, and at all the servants of king David: and all the people and all the mighty men were on his right hand and on his left. And thus said Shimei when he cursed, Come out, come out, thou bloody man, and thou man of Belial.

—2 Samuel 16:5–7, KJV

Shimei was calling David a worthless man. The Contemporary English Version says, "…you good-for-nothing." David was fleeing from his rebellious son, Absalom, when he encountered Shimei. Shimei was from the family of the house of Saul and was no doubt angry at the fact that David had succeeded Saul as king. This is just like the enemy to accuse God's anointed.

The Pharisees said Jesus cast out devils by Beelzebub. They were accusing Him of using Satan's power to deliver people. To call someone "a man of Belial" is to call that person worthless, no good, wicked, base, and vile. Shimei was accusing David of being a rebellious murderer who was responsible for Saul's fall. This is another example of how this spirit will attack and accuse the Lord's anointed.

> But Abishai the son of Zeruiah answered and said, "Shall not Shimei be put to death for this, *because he cursed the Lord's anointed*?"
> —2 Samuel 19:21, emphasis added

After David was returned to his position in Jerusalem, Shimei came to him and repented of what he said. Abishai desired to have him put to death for cursing the Lord's anointed. David, however, had mercy upon Shimei and did not put him to death.

David understood the judgment that would come upon those who touched the Lord's anointed. He refused to touch Saul even though his life was in danger. In the case of Shimei, mercy prevailed over judgment because of Shimei's *repentant* attitude.

Strong intercessors help cover the men and women of

God from the attacks of Belial. A *curse* is an evil work spoken against a person or a thing. Words spoken against the servants of God are spiritual arrows sent by the enemy to hurt and destroy. They are what the Word refers to as the "fiery darts of the wicked" (Eph. 6:16).

David understood the spiritual warfare the Lord's anointed must face when men curse. David prays in Psalm 64:2–3, "Hide me from the secret counsel of the wicked; from the insurrection of the workers of iniquity. Who whet their tongue like a sword, and bend their bows to shoot their arrows, even bitter words" (KJV).

These words are *witchcraft attacks* against the servants of the Lord. They are spiritual missiles directed toward the Lord's anointed. Life and death are in the power of the tongue (Prov. 18:21). This is one of the methods Belial uses to direct his assault against the servants of the Lord.

PRAYERS

PLOTS OF THE WICKED

Father, in their prideful, sinning ways, the wicked create plots to destroy the righteous. But You have promised, "The wicked in his pride persecutes the poor; let them be caught in the plots which they have devised" (Ps. 10:2).

Lord, the wicked plot continually to cause trouble and destruction to Your children. Your Word says that the wicked "sits in the lurking places of the villages; in the secret places he murders the innocent; his eyes are secretly fixed on the helpless" (Ps. 10:8). Lord, this describes the wicked plans of people today to spread the pain and sin of abortion. Shine the light of Your judgments upon the secretive, liberal attempts to lure young girls into a decision to abort the precious lives they are carrying. Stop the murder of the unborn, and cast this evil practice out of America.

Lord, Your Word describes the secret agenda of ungodly liberals to bind the poor into a lifestyle of dependence on others rather than independence and self-reliance. Your Word says, "He lies in wait secretly, as a lion in his den; he lies in wait to catch the poor; he catches the poor when he draws him into his net. So he crouches, he lies low, that the helpless may fall by his strength" (Ps. 10:9–10). Give us courage as Americans to become self-reliant, self-confident, and willing to be responsible for ourselves if possible rather than dependent on others.

Lord, like the writer of Proverbs, I feel as though I am being destroyed by the wicked plots of those who want to hurt me. But, like Solomon, my prayer is directed to You for Your grace and mercy: "I trust you,

LORD, and I claim you as my God. My life is in your hands. Save me from enemies who hunt me down. Smile on me, your servant. Have pity and rescue me. I pray only to you. Don't disappoint me. Disappoint my cruel enemies until they lie silent in their graves. Silence those proud liars! Make them stop bragging and insulting your people. You are wonderful, and while everyone watches, you store up blessings for all who honor and trust you. You are their shelter from harmful plots, and you are their protection from vicious gossip. I will praise you, LORD, for showing great kindness when I was like a city under attack. I was terrified and thought, 'They've chased me far away from you!' But you answered my prayer when I shouted for help. All who belong to the LORD, show how you love him. The LORD protects the faithful, but he severely punishes everyone who is proud. All who trust the LORD, be cheerful and strong" (Ps. 31:14–24, CEV).

THE WICKED WAR AGAINST THE GODLY

Lord, sometimes I feel just like David—surrounded by wickedness and threatened by destruction of my life. David cried out, saying, "Enemies are all around like a herd of wild bulls.... My enemies are like lions roaring and attacking with jaws open wide. I have no more strength than a few drops of water. All my bones are out of joint; my heart is like melted wax. My strength has dried up like a broken clay pot, and my tongue sticks to the roof of my mouth. You, God, have left me to die in the dirt. Brutal enemies attack me like a pack of dogs, tearing at my hands and my feet. I can count all my bones, and my enemies just stare and sneer at me....Don't stay far away, Lord!" (Ps. 22:12–17, 19, CEV). But, like David, I know this one thing: "My strength comes from you, so hurry and help" (v. 20, CEV).

David knew that You would come to his help, Lord, and so do I. I will follow the advice of Your Word: "Be patient and trust the Lord. Don't let it bother you when all goes well for those who do sinful things. Don't be angry or furious. Anger can lead to sin. All sinners will disappear, but if you trust the Lord, the land will be yours" (Ps. 37:7–9, CEV).

Father, Your Word describes a wicked person: "A worthless person, a wicked man, walks with a perverse mouth; he winks with his eyes, he shuffles his feet, he points with his fingers; perversity is in his heart, he devises evil continually, he sows discord. Therefore his calamity shall come suddenly; suddenly he shall be broken without remedy. These six things the Lord hates, yes, seven are an abomination to Him: a proud look, a lying tongue, hands that shed innocent blood, a heart that devises wicked plans, feet that are swift in running to evil, a false witness who speaks lies, and one who sows discord among brethren" (Prov. 6:12–19).

Father, I will strengthen my heart by praying these words from David: "Rescue me from cruel and violent enemies, LORD! They think up evil plans and always cause trouble. Their words bite deep like the poisonous fangs of a snake. Protect me, LORD, from cruel and brutal enemies who want to destroy me. Those proud people have hidden traps and nets to catch me as I walk. You, LORD, are my God! Please listen to my prayer. You have the power to save me, and you keep me safe in every battle. Don't let the wicked succeed in doing what they want, or else they might never stop planning evil. They have me surrounded, but make them the victims of their own vicious lies. Dump flaming coals on them and throw them into pits where they can't climb out. Chase those cruel liars away! Let trouble hunt them down. Our LORD, I know that you defend the homeless and see that the poor are given justice. Your people will praise you and will live with you because they do right" (Ps. 140, CEV).

GOD PROTECTS HIS ANOINTED

Father, even when David was being pursued by Saul, he refused to do anything that would harm Saul, who was Your anointed king over Israel. After he cut off a piece of Saul's robe in the cave, he stopped his men from hurting Saul, because Saul was the anointed servant of God: "And David arose and secretly cut off a corner of Saul's robe. Now it happened afterward that David's heart troubled him because he had cut Saul's robe. And he said to his men, 'The LORD forbid that I should do this thing to my master, the LORD's anointed, to stretch out my hand against him, seeing he is the anointed of the LORD.' So David restrained his servants with these words, and did not allow them to rise against Saul. And Saul got up from the cave and went on his way" (1 Sam. 24:4–7).

Father, again another time when David and Abishai stood before Saul as he slept, Abishai said, "'God has delivered your enemy into your hand this day. Now therefore, please, let me strike him at once with the spear, right to the earth; and I will not have to strike him a second time!' But David said to Abishai, 'Do not destroy him; for who can stretch out his hand against the LORD's anointed, and be guiltless?' David said furthermore, 'As the LORD lives, the LORD shall strike him, or his day shall come to die, or he shall go out to battle and perish. The LORD forbid that I should stretch out my hand against the LORD's anointed. But please, take now the spear and the jug of water that are by his head, and let us go.' So David took the spear and the jug of water by Saul's head, and they got away; and no man saw or knew it or awoke" (1 Sam. 26:8–12).

Father, help me to honor Your anointed servants just as David honored Saul.

Lord, when You made a covenant with Abraham, Isaac, and Jacob, You included this warning as a part of Your covenant: "Do not touch My anointed ones, and do My prophets no harm" (1 Chron. 16:22). May I always remember the value you place on Your anointed servants, and may I never do or say anything to dishonor them or to harm them.

Lord, Your Word promises, "Now I know that the LORD saves His anointed; He will answer him from His holy heaven with the saving strength of His right hand" (Ps. 20:6).

Father, David recognized that he was anointed by You and that You were the source of his strength. He praised You with these words: "The LORD is my strength and my shield; My heart trusted in Him, and I am helped; therefore my heart greatly rejoices, and with my song I will praise Him. The LORD is their strength, and He is the saving refuge of His anointed. Save Your people, and bless Your inheritance; shepherd them also, and bear them up forever" (Ps. 28:7–9).

CHAPTER 11

LOOSE YOURSELF FROM BELIAL'S CURSES

Verily I say unto you, Whatsoever ye shall bind on earth shall be bound in heaven: and whatsoever ye shall loose on earth shall be loosed in heaven.
—Matthew 18:18, KJV

Shake thyself from the dust; arise, and sit down, O Jerusalem: loose thyself from the bands of thy neck, O captive daughter of Zion.
—Isaiah 52:2, KJV

THIS IS A prophetic word to the church that says, "Loose thyself!" It is a powerful verse that relates to self-deliverance. We have been given the power and authority to loose ourselves from all types of bondage.

The word *loose* means "to disjoin, to divorce, to separate, asunder, sever, unhitch, disconnect, detach, unseat, unbind, unchain, unfetter, free, release, liberate, break up, break in pieces, smash, shatter, splinter, demolish, cleave, force apart." It also means "to forgive or pardon."

Zion is a prophetic word and symbol for the church. Isaiah prophesied that Zion would be a "captive daughter." This is so true of the condition of the church today. Even though many are saved and have received the promise of the Spirit, there are still many bondages that remain in the lives of believers.

SELF-DELIVERANCE

The question is often asked of me, "Can a person deliver himself of demons?" My answer is yes. It is also my conviction that a person cannot really keep himself free of demons until he is walking in this dimension of deliverance.

How is it that a person can deliver himself? As a believer (and that is our assumption), a person has the same authority as the believer who is ministering deliverance to another. He has the authority in the name of Jesus, and Jesus plainly promised those who believe, "In my name shall they cast out devils" (Mark 16:17, KJV).

Usually a person needs only to learn how to go about performing self-deliverance. After a person has experienced an initial deliverance at the hands of an experienced minister, he can begin to practice self-deliverance.*

---

* See Frank Hammond, *Pigs in the Parlor* (Kirkwood, MO: Impact Christian Books, 1973), 57.

The good news is that we have been given a prophetic promise and a command to loose ourselves. Jesus told His disciples that "whatsoever" we loose on Earth is loosed in heaven.

Whatsoever is binding, harassing, or operating in your life, contrary to the will of God, can be loosed from your life because you have been given the authority to do so.

The range of things that can bind a believer is almost limitless. There are many bondages we can categorize that need to be exposed and broken in the lives of all believers. Once you identify the enemy, you can then proceed to free yourself from his clutches.

LOOSE THYSELF FROM THE PAST

I have ministered to many believers who are still bound and tied to their past. The *past* can be a chain that keeps you from enjoying the present and being successful in the future.

While ministering deliverance to a young man, a strong spirit manifested who boasted that he would not depart. I commanded the spirit to identify himself, and he replied that his name was Past.

The spirit proceeded to explain that it was his job to keep the young man bound to his past so that he could not be successful in his Christian walk. The young man had been through a divorce, and his past continued to haunt him.

This encounter helped to give me a revelation of the fact

that there are numerous spirits assigned to people to keep them bound to the past that have left scars and wounds that have not completely healed. Many of these wounds have been infected and have become the dwelling places of unclean spirits. People need to be loosed not only from demons but also from other people. Ungodly soul ties are avenues spirits of control and manipulation utilize when working upon their unwary victims.

Prayer for Deliverance

Father, in Jesus's name, I loose myself from all relationships that are not ordained of God; all relationships that are not of the Spirit but of the flesh; all relationships based on control, domination, or manipulation; and all relationships based on lust and deception.

In the name of Jesus, I loose all members of my body, including my mind, memory, eyes, ears, tongue, hands, feet, and my entire sexual character, from all lust, perversion, sexual impurity, uncleanness, lasciviousness, promiscuity, pornography, fornication, homosexuality, fantasy, filthiness, burning passion, and uncontrollable sex drive.

I loose myself from the effects of all bad memories, painful memories, and memories of the past that would hinder me in the present or future.

I loose myself from all occult involvement, all sorcery, divination, witchcraft, psychic inheritance, rebellion, all confusion, sickness, death, and destruction as a result of occult involvement.

In the name of the Lord Jesus Christ, by the authority given to me to bind and loose, I loose my emotions from every evil spirit that has come in as a result of experiences of the past. I loose myself from all hurt, deep hurt, pain, sadness, grief, anger, hatred, rage, bitterness, fear, and bound and blocked emotions. I command these spirits to come out, and I decree freedom to my emotions in the name of Jesus.

I loose my mind from all spirits of mind control, confusion, mental bondage, insanity, madness, fantasy, passivity, intellectualism, knowledge block, ignorance, mind binding, lust, and evil thinking. I loose myself from all guilt, shame, condemnation, self-condemnation, and legalism.

I loose my will from all control domination and manipulation from Satan, his demons, and other people. I loose my will from all lust, rebellion, stubbornness, pride, self-will, selfishness, and antisubmissive spirits that block and hinder my will. I break and loose myself from all chains around my will, and I submit my will to the will of God.

CHAPTER 12

SAFE FROM the CURSE OF BELIAL

The path of the just is like the shining sun,
that shines ever brighter unto the perfect day.
The way of the wicked is like darkness; they
do not know what makes them stumble.
—Proverbs 4:18–19

FATHER, MAY I always remember the lessons You teach us in Proverbs 10, as You contrast the blessings for the righteous with the punishments for the wicked. These are Your promises to the righteous—and Your warnings to the wicked.

(Note: make a commitment to meditate each day of the coming month on one of these promises/punishments adapted from Proverbs 10.)

1. The Lord will not allow the righteous soul to famish, but He casts away the desire of the wicked.

2. He who has a slack hand becomes poor, but the hand of the diligent makes rich.

3. He who gathers in the summer is a wise son; he who sleeps in harvest is a son who causes shame.

4. Blessings are on the head of the righteous, but violence covers the mouth of the wicked.

5. The memory of the righteous is blessed, but the name of the wicked will rot.

6. The wise in heart will receive commands, but a prating fool will fall.

7. He who walks with integrity walks securely, but he who perverts his ways will become known.

8. He who winks with the eye causes trouble, but a prating fool will fall.

9. The mouth of the righteous is a well of life, but violence covers the mouth of the wicked.

10. Hatred stirs up strife, but love covers all sins.

11. Wisdom is found on the lips of him who has understanding, but a rod is for the back of him who is devoid of understanding.

12. Wise people store up knowledge, but the mouth of the foolish is near destruction.

13. The rich man's wealth is his strong city; the destruction of the poor is their poverty.

14. The labor of the righteous leads to life; the wages of the wicked, to sin.

15. He who keeps instruction is in the way of life, but he who refuses correction goes astray.

16. Whoever hides hatred has lying lips, and whoever spreads slander is a fool.

17. In the multitude of words sin is not lacking, but he who restrains his lips is wise.

18. The tongue of the righteous is choice silver; the heart of the wicked is worth little.

19. The lips of the righteous feed many, but fools die for lack of wisdom.

20. The blessing of the Lord makes one rich, and He adds no sorrow with it.

21. To do evil is like sport to a fool, but a man of understanding has wisdom.

22. The fear of the wicked will come upon him, and the desire of the righteous will be granted.

23. When the whirlwind passes by, the wicked is no more, but the righteous has an everlasting foundation.

24. As vinegar to the teeth and smoke to the eyes, so is the lazy man to those who send him.

25. The fear of the Lord prolongs days, but the years of the wicked will be shortened.

26. The hope of the righteous will be gladness, but the expectation of the wicked will perish.

27. The way of the Lord is strength for the upright, but destruction will come to the workers of iniquity.

28. The righteous will never be removed, but the wicked will not inhabit the earth.

29. The mouth of the righteous brings forth wisdom, but the perverse tongue will be cut out.

30. The lips of the righteous know what is acceptable, but the mouth of the wicked what is perverse.

The remaining chapters of Proverbs contain many more of these contrasted blessings for the righteous and punishments for the wicked. As an additional Bible study on righteousness contrasted with wickedness, continue selecting one contrast each day as your focus topic verse and prayer subject.

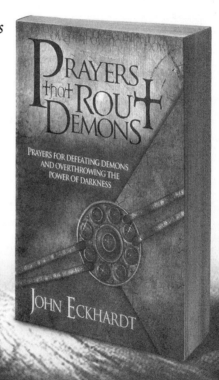